JOURNEY TO INDUSTRIAL & PRODUCT DESIGN

College Admissions & Profiles

Rachel A. Winston, Ph.D.

ISBN 978-1946432797 (hardback); 978-1946432780 (paperback); 978-1946432803 (e-book)

LCCN: 2022909855

Lizard Publishing, 7700 Irvine Center Drive, Suite 800, Irvine, CA 92618 *www.lizard-publishing.com*

Lizard Publishing creates, designs, produces, and distributes books and resources to provide academic, admissions, and career information. Our mental process is fueled by three tenets:

- Ignite the hunger to learn and the passion to make a difference
- Illuminate the expanse of knowledge by sharing cutting edge thinking
- Innovate to create a world that makes the transition from dreams to reality

We work with academic leaders who transform the educational landscape to publish relevant content and advise students of their educational and professional options, with the aim of developing 21st-century learners and leaders. We also work with students to publish their books and present widely diverse ideas to the college/graduate school-bound community. With headquarters in Irvine, California, Lizard Publishing works virtually with authors to edit, publish, and distribute both hard copy and paperback books.

This book was published in the U.S.A. Lizard Publishing is a premium quality provider of educational reference, career guidance, and motivational publications/merchandise for global learners, educators, and stakeholders in education.

Book design by Michelle Tahan *www.michelletahan.com*

Book formatting by Obinna Chinemerem Ozuo

Book website: *www.collegelizard.com*

LIZARD PUBLISHING

This book is dedicated to John Smart who never stopped innovating, imagining, and inventing a better future for society.

ACKNOWLEDGMENTS

There is never enough room to acknowledge every person. Numerous people contributed to my perspective about design and engineering. Students, faculty, counselors, and researchers assisted in enhancing my knowledge base or taught me indelible lessons. Over a lifetime of experiences working with students, I am wiser and more worldly.

I gratefully acknowledge Michelle Tahan, Jasmine Jhunjhnuwala, E. Liz Kim, Jacqueline Xu, and Chenoa Robbins as well as my family, friends, colleagues, and professors. With profound gratitude, I also acknowledge those I have known in the universes of design and engineering.

As a faculty member in the UCLA College Counseling Certificate Program, I met many dedicated counselors who spend their life serving and supporting students. Meaningful contributions to the book have been made indirectly by admissions representatives, college counselors, and faculty members who took a special interest in this book's success.

"If I see so far, it is because I stand on the shoulders of giants."
Isaac Newton

I would also like to thank the thousands of students I have taught, counseled, or supported in my nearly four decades of service.

Isaac Newton once said, "If I see so far, it is because I stand on the shoulders of giants." A few of those giants whose broad shoulders lifted me higher and helped teach invaluable lessons include Courtney Crisp, Bob Denton, Arman Ramezani, Fred Feldon, Mark Harbison, Gail Nichols, Karyn Holtzman, Rachel Sobel, Andrew Hunter, Ed Goul, JT Geehr, Barbara Pasalis, Shan Schumacher, Eric Hanzich, and Joe DeBilio.

Finally, there would be no book on Industrial and Product Design schools and no career in college admissions counseling without the support of Robert Helmer, whose tireless efforts support me every single day.

ABOUT THE AUTHOR

D r. Rachel A. Winston is a tireless student advocate. She has served the educational community as a university professor, college advisor, statistician, researcher, author, cryptanalyst, motivational speaker, publishing executive, and lifelong student. As one of the leading experts in college counseling and an award-winning faculty member, Dr. Winston has spent her lifetime learning, teaching, mentoring, and coaching students. Her counseling practice centers around college admissions, college essays, portfolios, and intellectual conversations about life and career pursuits.

She started college at thirteen and graduated from college programs in such widely ranging disciplines as chemistry, mathematics, computers, liberal arts, international relations, negotiation, conflict resolution, peacebuilding, business administration, higher education leadership, interpreting, college counseling, and publishing. Throughout her education, she attended and graduated from Harvard, University of Chicago, University of Texas, GWU, UCLA, Syracuse, CSUF, CSUDH, Pepperdine, Claremont Graduate University, and Gallaudet University.

Her position working in Washington, D.C. on Capitol Hill and with the White House in the 1980s took her to approximately a hundred universities training campaign managers at colleges from Colorado to California, thoroughly dotting the western states. Later, she led college tours with students and their families on road trips throughout the United States. She has taught or counseled thousands of students over her career and speaks at conferences and academic programs throughout the world.

As a professor and avid writer for numerous publications, she won the 2012 McFarland Literary Achievement Award, Bletchley Park Cryptanalyst Award, and numerous other awards, including Faculty Member of the Year, Leadership Tomorrow Leader of the Year, and college service and leadership awards. While studying Human Capital at Claremont Graduate University, she was a scholarship recipient at the Drucker School of Management. She was also elected to the statewide Board of Governors for the Faculty Association for California Community Colleges, where she served on the executive committee.

She also served as a faculty member for the UCLA College Counselor Certificate Program, the Director of Mathematics at Brandman University, and Embry Riddle Aeronautical University, Chapman University, Cal State Fullerton, and a handful of California Community Colleges, including Cerro Coso College where she represented the entire faculty as the Academic Senate President and retired in 2016. Over her career, she taught mathematics online, on television, live interactive satellite, telecourses, and in large and small lecture halls.

AUTHOR'S NOTE

You are reading this book because you are considering admission to colleges where you open the doors to the world of design, engineering, and creativity. Whatever route you took to get to this point, you are in the right place. Right now, you need to gather information to make informed decisions.

While many people offer advice, suggestions differ. Friends will tell you the 'right' way or the way their neighbor was accepted. Graciously accept this anecdotal information, pursuing imaginative artistry with your heart and mind as you commit to learning more.

Dig deeper to consider both expert and current information from counselors who have worked with hundreds of students. Changes in programs, curricula, requirements, and links happen each year.

Doublecheck each program's specifics yourself. Each school's profile information is current as of April 2022. However, since researching this book, changes may have taken place. There are other college guidebooks written by talented and experienced counselors, though none like this book on college programs for product and industrial design. Nevertheless, I admire and cheer on their efforts.

"We are what we think. All that we are arises with our thoughts. With our thoughts, we make the world."
Buddha

This book, providing lists of colleges, admissions information, and profiles, is different in that it also offers unique tidbits. I hope you find the information valuable. Your job is to begin early by assembling lists of possible schools to consider. Create a road map and set yourself on a clear path.

If you see an error in this book or even a suggestion for a future edition, please write to Dr. Rachel A. Winston at collegeguide@yahoo.com. We will fix the entry with the next printed version. All of that said, this book was written with you in mind.

This book contains a wealth of information on the Internet with free downloads, FAQs, testimonials, and offers to help you with your applications. Some of these advisors are knowledgeable and provide valuable assistance. Unfortunately, students and parents hunt around the web, searching for a tremendous number of hours to seek the information they need. This book aims to resolve this problem with college admissions data and profiles to make your search easier.

For now, though, I will assume you want to attend college to study product and industrial design and are exploring this book to find a program that will get you on your way toward your goal. You are undoubtedly a talented candidate who is willing to work very hard. Creative mental exploration is virtually a prerequisite for design programs.

As you investigate colleges, you might find that some programs are listed in art, design, engineering, or liberal arts departments. Either way, this book will help you reach your goal. Applying to and writing essays for each application will require research to determine which program is right for you and the specific reasons you are a good fit.

While you might believe that design-focused colleges are relatively similar, each program's nuances make them very different. These small differences may seem confusing. My goal with this book is to demystify the information and process.

CONTENTS

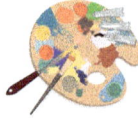

CHAPTER 1

ENVISION, DESIGN, & PRODUCE: INNOVATING PRODUCTS, PACKAGES, & TOOLS

"You can't use up creativity. The more you use, the more you have."

– Maya Angelou

Have you ever wanted to redesign your keyboard, chair, cell phone, bicycle, skateboard, or game? Have you seen prototypes of next-gen phones that seamlessly see, talk, write, compute, follow your route, and a host of other functions in a gadget the size of a credit card? Well, new inventions are coming, and they are cool! Industrial Designers lead society on the cutting-edge of product design to make life simpler and more efficient.

Industrial Designers are inventors and idea-generators. They take a client's general idea, visualize its structure, design the item, and then bring the idea to fruition. Startups need their designs engineered and crafted for consumer use. Individuals or groups envision a uniquely designed drone, robot, solar car, VR set, toy, game, shoe, or everyday household item. Taking the idea from concept to design, requires them to be drawn, designed, modeled, tested, and manufactured. Ultimately, efficient, effective products emerge to generate millions in sales.

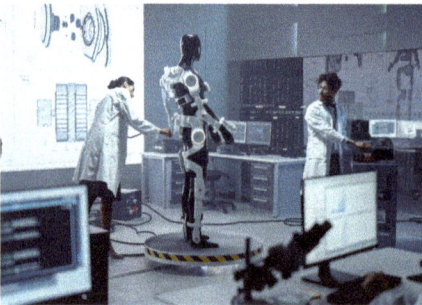

INDUSTRIAL AND PRODUCT DESIGN

Industrial Design is the professional service of creating products and systems that optimizes function, value, safety, appearance, and sustainability for the mutual benefit of the user, manufacturer, and the planet. Nearly every object imaginable was once modeled by an Industrial/Product Designer. The field of Industrial Design is essentially today's modernized version of Product Design.

The terms Product Design and Industrial Design are relatively interchangeable since they perform the same function, even though some colleges have established programs emphasizing one versus the other. When there is a difference, Industrial Design typically leans more toward engineering, while Product Design often leans more toward departments of architecture, design, or art. Nevertheless, despite their seemingly different paths, they converge at the same point in designing products.

Industrial and Product Designers are a cross between engineers and artists. Considering the product's ideal outcome, they take into account the human element as they sketch, draft, and model the item from concept to consumer purchase.

ACADEMIC REQUIREMENTS AND TECHNICAL SKILLSETS

Being good at chemistry, physics, and calculus in high school is just the beginning. You need to enjoy the 3D design process, from sketches to computer modeling to 3D printing. While in high school, you should seek solid experiences in drawing, programming, robotics, and engineering during your summers. You might join a robotics, engineering, or computer club in school. You might take studio art or a college class focused on Adobe Illustrator or Adobe Photoshop. Sketching is an invaluable skill in this major. A few schools even require an artistic portfolio.

You can gain the skills you need to know in college. However, students say that learning to draw proficiently or program quickly while taking difficult science and engineering classes and developing complex, innovative projects is like drinking through a firehose. After a professor's brief introduction to a topic, you are on your own. You will need to teach yourself how to progress through a project and create a prototype from concept to completion, often without a lot of help.

Simplicity is the ultimate sophistication.

– From Apple's first brochure

So, what skills do you need to succeed in this field?
- Drawing, design, and measurement
- Visualization of objects in 3D and creating prototypes
- Imagination, innovation, and modernization
- Love for building things – think Legos on steroids
- Eager anticipation for VR, AR, and machine learning
- Analytical thinking with a physics mindset
- Quick thinking and problem solving
- Computer software navigation
- Organization and time management
- Perception, intuition, and ability to understand customer's needs
- Business-mindedness regarding cost, budget, and accounting

Industrial Designers typically have a bachelor's or master's degree in Industrial Design, Product Design, architecture, or engineering. To apply for a position, students must develop a digital portfolio of Industrial Design projects which they share with companies. From start to finish Industrial Designers work with customers to bring their ideas to fruition. In the process of doing so industrial designers

- Learn the needs of clients.
- Bid on contracts with individuals, startups, or companies.
- Consult with customers to determine design requirements.
- Determine pain points – What problem is this product attempting to solve?
- Research demographics of target audiences.
- Examine data regarding current/expected uses, utility, and functionality.
- Sketch ideas, develop renderings, and create digital models.
- Produce physical prototypes for clients to test and examine.
- Work with mechanical/manufacturing engineers to analyze design concepts.
- Consider ergonomics, haptics, safety, appearance, and sustainability.
- Evaluate materials, manufacturing, and production costs.
- Present designs, demonstrate prototypes, and test functionality with clients.
- Register patents to legally protect inventions.
- Travel, following through with the design and production process to ensure success.

HUMAN-CENTERED DESIGN

Have you ever thought about the many ways humans live their lives and the challenges some face? When you work in human-centered design, you need to consider everything - height, weight, strength, grip, mobility, body construction, athleticism, disability, age, weakness, heat, cold, humidity, space, technical ability, and a host of other situations that might impact a product's use.

A chair is an excellent example of a product that is used universally. Chair height alone is a critical factor in designing an airplane seat, followed by the challenge of sufficient legroom. Over a person's lifetime, most people have sat in chairs that were too high, too low, or extremely uncomfortable. Especially for those people who sit in a room or office for long hours in a day, finding the right chair is essential. Industrial Designers attempt to reimagine ways to offer customers chairs that better fit their needs at a price they can afford to pay.

While sitting is a unifying behavior, chairs come in hundreds of styles for a myriad of uses – school, home, office, medicine, massage, restaurant, beach, car, train, plane, swing set, tailgate party, park bench, etc. Industrial Designers consider comfort, value, ergonomics, aesthetics, material, shape, utility, breathability, sustainability, and ability to heat, cool, vibrate, lift, swivel, and roll.

Human-centered product design needs to focus on the corporate client and discerning customer. Spatial thinking and 3D design must be considered in light of the myriad of ways the product may be used as well as both expected and unexpected environmental conditions. In other words, the Industrial Designer must think about what a kid would do with an object made for an adult. What would happen in the case of a sudden electrical surge, water damage from a hurricane, or a child taking the object apart?

The product must also be considered within a system of other items. For example, let's say you were designing a bookcase. The project seems simple. You want to create a shelving system for books. You can analyze the size of typical books and those atypical ones that may also need to fit on the shelf. While there are standard sizes, there is considerable wasted space if the shelves are too high.

You then need to consider the weight of the books that may be packed into the bookcase and whether the shelves would buckle or sag over time if the shelf was packed with books. Then, you might consider, what if the person does not put books on the shelf? What if they put a solid metal statue? What if a child crawled into the space just for fun and banged into the shelf above that had the heavy metal statue? This kind of holistic thinking goes into each product, attending to the finest details and considerations that might otherwise be ignored.

CONSUMER ELECTRONICS SHOW

If you ever have the chance to go to the Consumer Electronics Show (CES) in Las Vegas – GO! The event takes place during the first week of January each year. More than 100,000 people attend with vendors from across the globe. For an Industrial Designer, the dozens of massive showroom floors can be more fun than Disneyland.

The show features just about every invention and prototype imaginable. The nonstop awe is literally breathtaking. I went every year before the pandemic. Each year was equally as amazing as any previous year. Extraordinary cutting-edge products will make you stare in awe while giving you hundreds of ideas for novel products. Besides the sports, camera, household, drone, and robotic devices, one of those products that mesmerized people was the 3-D printers.

THE ROAD TO INDUSTRIAL DESIGN

Industrial Designers are multidimensional thinkers. They consider products from different angles, cross-sections, and durability, conductivity, and strength of possible materials. Some specialize in a type of product like appliances, furniture, or surfboards. With the client's specifications in mind, they create, drawing on long tables, brainstorming notes on whiteboards, diligently calibrating digital designs, and prototyping concept models with the latest high-tech equipment.

Meanwhile, Industrial Designers work with engineers to ensure that designs can be produced efficiently and result in the optimum value and utility. Often Industrial Designers must compete for projects, travel to present their vision, and then design, test, support, and ensure the proper manufacture and function.

The road to becoming an Industrial or Product Designer is not necessarily longer than other fields, but it requires a special type of person who loves problem-solving and is undaunted by challenges. Some of those challenges include getting up to speed with Adobe Creative Cloud, Solidworks (3D CAD), or AutoCAD. For automotive design, you may need to learn Autodesk's Alias sketching, modeling, surfacing, and visualization or its Fusion 360 for CAD/CAM/CAE to design, test, and fabricate. Another software for automotive design is Siemens NX for Design. While some of these options are expensive, there are free Industrial Design software tools as well.

To create a prototype, you need to start with a sketch. However, a 2D sketch needs to translate into 3D via software. You may also want to animate your product on a screen so you can 'demonstrate' how the design would function. Many production teams use whiteboard, collaboration, or task/project management software. There are literally dozens in every price range and utility.

Whatever you design – a car, airplane part, motor, robot, toy, or chair - will be new and better. You are only limited by your imagination.

Design is not just what it looks like and feels like. Design is how it works.

– Steve Jobs

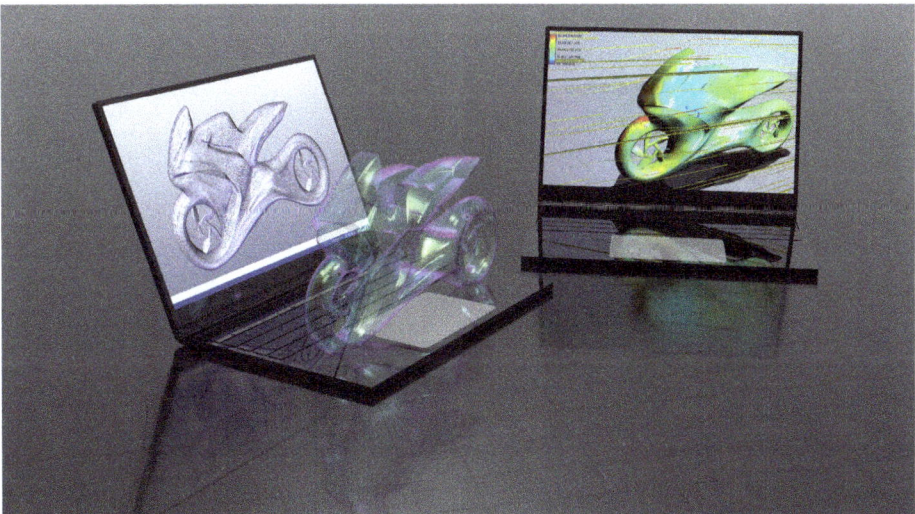

CHAPTER 2

THE ART & SCIENCE OF TECHNICAL DESIGN: PAST, PRESENT, AND FUTURE

"Give thanks for everything that happens to you, knowing that every step forward is a step toward achieving something bigger and better than your current situation."

— **Brian Tracy**

From apes to Neanderthals to Homo Sapiens, the legacy of Industrial Design began with cutting and molding to create cooking and hunting tools. 'Designed', 'redesigned', and reimagined over the next few millennia, early humans began to hunt, cook, and eat, using materials and constructions developed with the 'high technology' of the day. Albeit, these items are not the high-tech products we have in the 21st-century but, put yourself in their shoes, they did the best they had living in the jungle with only stones, wood, mud, leaves, twine, vines, fruit, and animals.

Living in caves or huts, they began their journey into fabrication and molding. They soon transformed hides, furs, and leaves into rudimentary clothing. Artisans used form, shape, and function to craft bowls, vessels, and tools.

Adornments came soon after with jewelry, symbols, and embellishments, giving birth to fashion design. Watch out Giorgio Armani, Coco Chanel, Calvin Klein, Marc Jacobs, Ralph Lauren, and Donatella Versace! These early hunters and gatherers, our inquisitive ancestors, were on their way to the 21st-century.

Skillbuilding led to crafts, which in turn led to trades. Quite a few thousand years ago there were specialists in stone toolmaking, hide production, ornamental design, pottery craftsmanship, fire building, wood carving, hunting tools, and epicurean treats. Metalworkers came next as did shipbuilders. Okay, maybe they started with rafts, but navigating a river, lake, or sea was very important for transportation.

Experimenting with lightweight materials, buoyancy, and binding options, 'research' was required. Every new product developed a few millennia ago needed to be tested, remodeled, and retested. Horses offered excellent transportation and cows were strong enough to plough fields and develop agriculture. Their milk was good to drink; their meat served as an excellent source of protein; and their hides were used for shoes, jackets, and containers. Additionally, the manure they left behind also help the crops thrive. Who knew? Humans were off to the races, ready for the next societal transformation.

A few thousand years ago thatched-roofed buildings were commonplace as were methods for primitive airflow, heating, cooling, water, food, and lifestyle. Over time, cities became enclaves for craftspeople who produced a variety of goods. The printing press allowed for the transmission of information as scientific progress gained steam - literally. The Renaissance transformed medicine, politics, art, and life. However, handcrafted items, made individually, were extremely expensive.

Steel and steam transformed society into the burgeoning industrial revolution. Mass-production allowed manufacturing to be automated. Industrialization took off with reductions in costs and production time. Efficiencies allowed for the quick construction and assembly of furniture, musical instruments, and household items. Millions of people could now access goods never before readily available to the average family.

The 1851 London World Exposition was sponsored by the first soft drink company, Schweppes. This major event revealed artisan-made, intricately designed objects like pianos, sewing machines, telescopes, the Jacquard loom, kitchen appliances, and a reaping machine. An innovation explosion had begun.

People like John Ruskin pushed back on the division of labor, believing that factory-made work was "dishonest" as "craftsmanship". In 1861, William Morris, who adopted Ruskin's philosophy, is considered the leading force behind the Arts and Crafts Movement, using craftsmanship to consider design and function. From 1890 to 1910 Art Nouveau took hold, rejecting the industrial revolution's mass production and, instead, inspiring new forms of art.

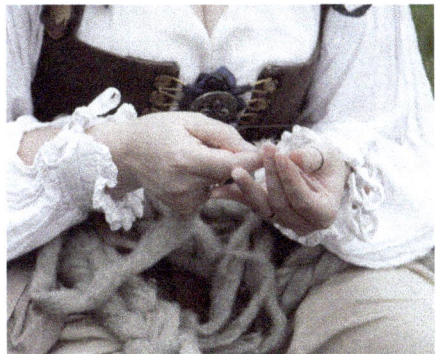

20TH-CENTURY INDUSTRIAL DESIGN

Industrial Design is considered a 20th-century field, started by German architect Peter Behrens. In 1903 Austria, *Wiener Werkstatte* (Vienna's Workshops) opened, bringing together architects, designers, and artisans to design distinctive items in a pioneering effort to handcraft metals, leather, bookbinding, furniture, textiles, and ceramics.

Peter Behrens trained as a painter and was heavily influenced by art nouveau. He designed groundbreaking architecture that was considered unpretentious, impressive, and sophisticated. He also invented numerous products. He was influential in the founding of Deutsche Werkbund in 1907, the German association of artists, architects, and designers which began the mass production of industrial designs, crafts, and other tools. In the interwar period, the Bauhaus school of design grew in Weimar Germany as the Germans ramped up their efforts to rebuild after World War I.

Design is not about decorating functional forms – it is about creating forms that accord with the character of the object and that show new technologies to advantage.
— **Peter Behrens**

AMERICAN INDUSTRIAL DESIGN MOVEMENT

Society transformed in a big way as workshop crafts became mass-produced. Factories produced cars, trains, boats, buses, and streetcars, which transported people from one place to another more efficiently than the horse. The U.S. Patent Office officially recognized the term Industrial Designer in 1913 as inventions proliferated with the ingenuity of leaders in the field like Norman Bel Gedes, Henry Dreyfuss, Raymond Loewy, Donald Deskey, and Walter Dorwin Teague.

In the United States, Norman Bel Gedes, considered one of America's Industrial Design pioneers, opened an Industrial Design studio in 1927, where he designed commercial products, theatrical sets, airliners, radio cabinets, Mark 1 computer case, and unrealized futuristic technologies. He is famous for designing the Motors Futurama building at the 1939 New York World's Fair.

Henry Dreyfuss worked as an apprentice to Norman Bel Gedes, opening his own Industrial Design studio in 1929. He designed the "phone of the future" for Bell Laboratories, a deluxe refrigerator for General Electric, an alarm clock for Westclox, a vacuum cleaner for Hoover, steam engines and cars for the railroads, and a washing machine for Sears. He later served as the President of the Industrial Designers Society of America (IDSA). He is best known for his work in ergonomics.

Although the Industrial Design movement started in Austria and Germany, the 'Father of Industrial Design' is considered to be Raymond Loewy who designed everything from the Coca-Cola bottle and Sears refrigerator to the Studebaker automobile and railroad terminals. He crossed industries from designing the razor to branding famous images like the Lucky Strike cigarette packet, Quaker, Nabisco, Shell Oil, TWA, Exxon, and the U.S. Postal Service. Raymond Loewy brought elegant design to the masses as companies realized the importance of the combination of design, efficiency, utility, cost, and functionality.

The ideas and inventions of these and others like Donald Deskey, designer of Radio City Music Hall's interior, and Walter Dorwin Teague, the designer of Kodak cameras, Pringles canister, and Boeing airliner interiors. Each of these pioneers led the way in the field of Industrial Design, aided by the early 1900s development of materials like vinyl, chrome, aluminum, and plywood. Montgomery Ward formed in-house Industrial Design departments followed by Sears, IBM, General Motors, and Electrolux as the field expanded.

Industrial Designers crossed lines between engineer and artist. Yet, with the growing belief, suggested by the "father of skyscrapers" and architect Louis Sullivan that "form follows function", the purpose of Industrial Design shifted to ergonomics, engineering, innovation, and manufacturing.

MODERN INDUSTRIAL DESIGNERS

Central to Industrial Design today exists a vision of creativity and ingenuity. Exciting new products are being conjured, developed, and manufactured to improve society. Within a given brand-focused theme, these products offer greater efficiency and effectiveness by harnessing ergonomics, shape, tactical haptics, color, materials, finishings, manufacturing, and function.

Most Industrial Design studios are composed of collaborative interdisciplinary teams. With training in varied and multiple areas from design to business, user interface (UI) designers and user experience (UX) designers come together with project managers, customers, and manufacturers to achieve common goals. To be sure, the initial prototype is rarely the last, so some of the design work rests in making, breaking, reconfiguring, testing materials, and scanning remotely possible outcomes.

Each item we use impacts our life, our space, and our efficiency. Industrial Designers consider today's space design and environment. Some people today live in New York City apartments no larger than a typical business office. Thus, printers, refrigerators, microwave ovens, heaters, air conditioners, alarm clocks, etc. need to be smaller, lighter, and moveable. Thus, an Industrial Designer needs to sense the needs of the consumer and feel their lived experience whether that life is in New York City, rural Alabama, frosty Fairbanks, Alaska, or points overseas in Europe, Africa, Asia, or South America.

Design is the fundamental soul of a human-made creation.

– Steve Jobs

TODAY'S INDUSTRIAL DESIGN OPPORTUNITIES

Today, the world faces significant spatial, electronic, and transportation challenges. Intelligent, human-centered design thinking is essential to resolve living, learning, technological, and supply chain problems. Smart, broad-minded Industrial Designers gain the multidimensional training necessary for research, rendering, and fabrication. In turn, they will produce, test, and present solutions.

Remember that everything in our sphere exists in a system. Interfaces and functionality must make sense within the environment. Thus, Industrial Designers must be aware of people's surroundings and what might support or interfere with functionality. For example, drones may repair our supply chain issues, but what disturbances, errors, or nefarious challenges must be considered. Medical equipment technologies may save a person's life, but could the materials be rejected from the human body. What other solutions might make industrial work safer, cleaner, healthier, and more productive? And, considering sustainability, are the products environmentally friendly?

In a metal fabrication workshop, you will mold, laser cut, and weld your material, testing out rapid prototyping. In the modeling shop, you will experiment with foam, plastic, and wood. A woodshop project may require that you create an ergonomic chair to code and safety specifications, adding upholstery and backings that fit your design concept. When working on your transportation design project, you will use design software to convert sketches and orthographic drawings into renderings. You will create innovative toys for children, presenting your vision and prototype in a presentation. You might even translate your ideas into the next cool toy.

From your first-year experiences to sponsored workshops, studios are abuzz with activity. You will survey consumer needs, translating proposals from concepts to physical products using aesthetic appeal and engineering design. There are no limits to what you can imagine. Then, you can decide what you choose to create - game consoles, phones, cars, computers, or healthcare items. You may train in auxiliary skills like interaction or entertainment design, mass production, or manufacturing. Avoid the steep learning curves by taking design courses from the moment you think you might be interested in this pursuit.

You will also need to know the law. When you are protecting your inventions with a patent, you need to be extremely detailed and understand the nuances of intellectual property. College will push you into the deep end, but you will learn how to swim using your instincts and problem-solving skills to make products more functional and attractive. However, your ideas about how to improve society will become reality.

Emerging technologies, UX design, and interaction design will force you to swim faster to say ahead of the next wave of new tools coming your way. Augmented Reality (AR) and Virtual Reality (VR) opportunities are here. Their full force implementation is right around the corner.

When I am working on a problem, I never think about beauty. But when I have finished, if the solution is not beautiful, I know it is wrong.

- R. Buckminster Fuller

CHAPTER 3

CHAPTER 3

ENGINEERING HIGH-TECH PRODUCTS: ADVANCED SKILLS TO DESIGN NEXT-GEN TECHNOLOGIES

"A flower does not think of competing to the flower next to it. It just blooms."

– Zen Shin

TECHNOLOGY'S FUTURE IS AROUND THE CORNER

Technology is continually evolving, adapting, and improving. As a result, an enormous transformation is taking place in the digital environment that will likely alter much of what we know and do today. You will be at the forefront of emerging technologies appearing within the next decade. With Internet speeds up to one hundred times faster in the span of ten years, the power and promise of visual imagery will change life as we know it.

Digital optimization within the spaces of 5G, 6G, and 7G will advance Industrial Design and consumer products in revolutionary rather than evolutionary ways. Computing power, many times faster than today, will allow for quick permutations of design options, images, and animations never before possible. In addition, designers and other professionals will collaborate on holograms in shared spaces with members who need not be physically present.

Models, prototypes, animations, and videos bring the future to life today by telling stories that people can understand. I must have watched the now decade-old Corning Glass company's video "A Day Made of Glass" a few dozen times. Watching each vision come to fruition today is breathtaking. Though conceptualized a while ago, I remain duly impressed. Your job is to project how you see the world transitioning and project that vision through the products you design, turning them into the story of tomorrow, much like Corning did in its video.

Clearly visualized animations using virtual reality will allow customers and patrons to experience what has not yet been created. Augmented reality will add to this experience by providing the viewer a user experience, possibly, one day, in the Metaverse. Stories will be told in new spaces and environments with fully automated computer design and programming tools. Group members will be able to adapt works for publication or showcase imagery in quick iterations, allowing for a near-real representation as each person analyzes the form and function within a digital gallery or pages of a text.

METAVERSE

The Metaverse will be a dynamic living-working environment by 2030. It's not that far off now. Developers are constructing homes, offices, and even clothing for this digital space. While second life was an introduction, where people dabbled into holding lectures in the digital world, today, tremendously successful concerts have been held in the Metaverse, and that is just the beginning. How this impacts Industrial Design and product development is up to your imagination. However, other people are on the trail of making this experiential realm a reality sooner than you think.

Big brand names have entered this space in full force. Luxury clothing designers are creating fashions for their elite clientele. Big infrastructure construction companies are building roads, office buildings, shopping centers, and stores. Lawyers are buying offices for negotiation, mediation, and litigation. While there is much work to be done before this transition, one thing is certain, there will be some fascinating products bought and sold through this platform. See you there!

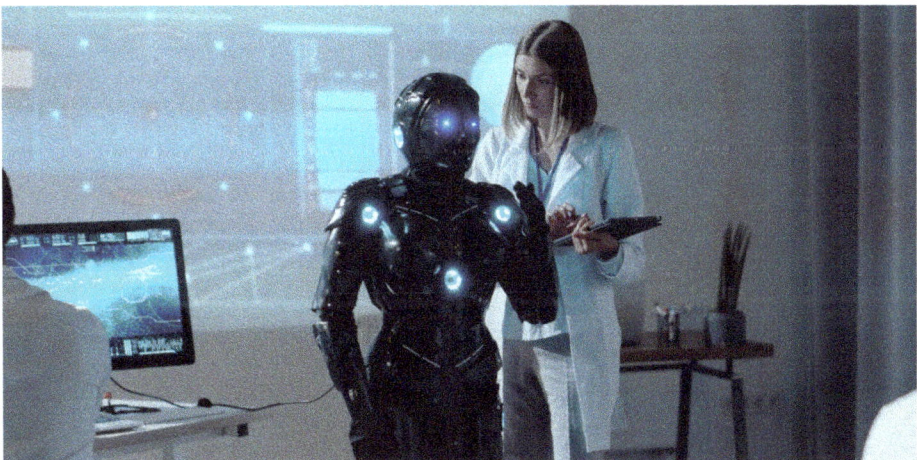

Haptics is another area where the future will unfold. Haptics is the science of human touch. If we can resolve how touch happens and create synthetic touch devices, a robot can open a door handle, replace an ink cartridge, or bring us our favorite sweater. Thus, haptics' ability to sense and operate machinery or complete ordinary tasks will change the products we design today. This ability will also change video game, virtual reality, and augmented reality experiences by making controllers more sensitive.

Movers and shakers who imagine and develop these consumer engagement technologies are likely to be very successful. This concept is not sci-fi. Touchable, wearable, and infotainment systems are here-and-now science. Vibration-sensored, button stimulation, thermal control, and kinesthetic devices are on the market today. Universities are hotly researching haptics for force, tactile, and proprioceptive feedback.

Proprioceptive refers to the stimuli that sense distance, weight, effort, and position for appropriate movement. If we can resolve how humans know where to scratch an itch, how hard to kick a ball, or when to pull up their socks, we can create products with these abilities. We may also be able to receive instantaneous device responses, relaying information quickly back to the user. However, haptics also offers simpler near-term design possibilities with mechanical interfaces as well.

ROBOTS, DRONES, AND FLYING MACHINES

During the pandemic, robots walked dogs, and delivered medicines to patients in hospitals for contactless delivery. Other types of contactless options devised during the pandemic included deliver boxes, self-driving vehicles, tracked packaging, and food/grocery deliveries.

Automated drone technologies are changing the way packages are delivered. For example, Zipline, an American medical product delivery company based in San Francisco, delivered medical supplies, blood, and vaccines to rural Rwanda and Ghana. In 30 minutes, deliveries can be made in what used to take an entire day, reducing traffic, pollution, delivery time, and transportation costs. The market for drone delivery is expected to reach almost 10 billion dollars in the next five years. For comparison, the entire movie and video industry in the U.S. in 2022 is $18.2 billion.

Here are the top ten drone delivery companies in 2022.

- Prime Time Air
- FedEx
- UPS Flight Forward
- DHL Parcelcopter
- Wing
- Matternet
- Zipline
- Flytrex
- Flirtey
- Wingcopter

On the island of Cyprus, a man instructed his drone to walk his dog when the country went on lockdown. Drones are used in crime surveillance, warehouse inventory, search and rescue, and disaster response. With its ability to monitor wildfires, conflict zones, and national borders, drones make an excellent replacement for helicopters. Farmers can check crops over large areas and between crops where vehicles cannot maneuver.

Drone journalism offers new opportunities for flyover image capture, providing photographic and sound information to be transferred from flying devices to users in ways never before seen. Virtual and augmented reality will further integrate into society.

Today's pioneering engineers use visionary foresight and transformative power to design digital worlds, opening the doors for Industrial Designers to experiment with image-capturing sensory devices, possibly where people can one day feel and experience what they see. Thus, the potential to have a multisensory experience may require 'cameras' with new components yet to be invented. With new technologies, innovative products could be on the cutting-edge of how society reimagines sensory experiences.

INDUSTRIAL DESIGN INVENTIVENESS

Ferrari's quick-thinking innovators used 3D printing to convert snorkels into respirators. Ferrari converted its prototype vehicle area into a 3D printing section to produce thermoplastic valves designed to fit facemask snorkeling devices. These respirators were delivered to hospitals throughout Italy.

Successful products through 2030 will be locally produced, personalized, safe, sustainable, and tastefully crafted using human-centered design. People are clamoring for easy-to-use wireless products that are transportable and filled with smart features like voice control. People seek eco-friendly designs using biodegradable materials with a commitment to carbon neutrality, pollution reduction, and sustainability. Artificial intelligence will lead the way toward simplicity and minimalism. People want to interact more with their environment using scannable codes, augmented reality, and voice assistants.

MATERIAL SCIENCE

Chemistry may seem dry, pardon the pun, but there is an immense amount of research transforming the materials to use in your product development. Carbon is one of the hottest elements in the research sphere today. So, when graphene grabbed people's attention, researchers clamored to discover its many uses. Graphene is a one-atom-thick sheet of carbon that conducts heat and electricity along its plane, absorbs light of all visible wavelengths, is 100 times stronger than the strongest steel, and is nearly transparent.

The possibilities for graphene's uses are endless, including building materials, electronics, transportation, and military. Companies have already begun using offshoots of this to build the foundations of buildings and computer screens that will lay flat on your wall. You could be part of some very big and profitable innovations.

In 2010, two Russian scientists were awarded the Nobel Prize in Physics for their discovery and groundbreaking research uses for graphene. This nanomaterial offers high tensile strength, electrical conductivity, and transparency. Earlier, in 1996, two Americans and one British researcher won the Nobel Prize in Chemistry for their discoveries regarding another carbon-based molecule.

Fullerene, C60, has similarly fascinating properties with a tremendous number of possible uses for nanotubes, nanorods, and other nanotechnologies like tumor therapy. Presently researchers believe that C60 is not only an antioxidant, but the molecule has healing properties that may slow down aging, boost immunity, increase energy, reduce wrinkles, inhibit fat cell production, and provide stronger mental capacity.[1]

New synthetic leathers may be better for clothing, footwear, steering wheel covers, seats, bags, furnishings, sports, and electronics. Liquid and spray camouflage coatings may have utility for some defense, aircraft, and clothing products. Aspheric lenses are low in cost and high in performance, offering high-end optical solutions with sharper images and reduced optical imperfections for cameras, camera phones, CD players, and reading glasses.

With concerns for safety, flame retardant coatings might be important. Another wonder material is spider silk which is more flexible than nylon and thinner than human hair. Spider silk can be used for medical purposes as well as for bulletproof vests since it can absorb three times as much energy as Kevlar. However, since spider silk is biodegradable, its properties might make it the right eco-friendly material for parachutes, ropes, seatbelts, bandages, artificial tendons, or rust-free boat accessories.

Since there are quite literally thousands of amazing materials and products on the cutting edge of idea generation, the future is in your hands. The potential is limitless to reduce, reuse, recycle, and create. How do you imagine the future? I hope this chapter got you thinking before you embark on your dynamic educational experiences in college.

Go for it!

---

1   Rebecca Suhrawardi. "This Nobel Prize-Winning Molecule Could Be the Best Thing For Anti-Aging." *Forbes*, April 30, 2021. https://www.forbes.com/sites/rebeccasuhrawardi/2021/04/30/this-nobel-prize-winning-molecule-could-be-the-best-thing-for-anti-aging/?sh=2d7fa2ca6ada

CHAPTER 4

INDUSTRIAL & PRODUCT DESIGN: ACADEMIC PREPARATION & CAREER OPTIONS

"Tell me and I forget. Teach me and I remember. Involve me and I learn."

– Benjamin Franklin

THE COLLEGE EXPERIENCE IN INDUSTRIAL DESIGN

Studying Industrial Design will challenge you in multiple ways, but you will never be bored. You will draw, use design software, and prepare models on prototyping machinery. You will work together with others, and you will work alone. If you like drawing, crafting, modeling, casting, molding, and printing, you will get plenty of practice. Expect to pull a few all-nighters. You will not be alone in the studio on the nights before projects are due.

Collaboration is at the core of Industrial Design. You will not only work on projects with people in your major, but you are likely to consult with students in mechanical engineering, electrical engineering, industrial engineering, and material science.

You will also need to be practically obsessed with inspecting fine details since the smallest accidental notch or defective metal piece will hang your project out to dry. If you do not find those details, trust me, your professors will – every last design flaw.

You will continually identify and resolve challenges. Thus, the two most important academic skills you will need as an Industrial Design student are problem-solving and critical thinking. Consider alternative possibilities and get feedback, even if you are worried that the critique may be harsh. The alternative is a low grade or a defective product. After a product is mass-produced in large.

ACADEMIC PREPARATION

You are headed toward the mastery of Industrial and Product Design: To gain admission to your dream college, you must be smart and talented. Even if the

admissions requirements do not require a portfolio, to be successful, you must develop numerous preparatory skills as if you were presenting your drawings or design work to a committee—plan for your future now. Talent is only the beginning.

You must build solid skills inside and outside of high school or college to enter a program. The more exceptional academic skills, coursework, standardized tests, or artwork you present to an admissions committee, within their guidelines, the better. Take advantage of engineering, computer, or robotics camps. Try classes in drawing, 3-D design, 3-D printing, engineering, robotics, digital art, photography, or animation. Some applicants have never taken these classes and are not penalized, but these skills are extremely helpful. Nevertheless, foundational skills are important.

The freedom to create designs compels people to pursue this field, though the reality is that working on projects for other people can be stressful. On the other hand, if you owned a design firm, you could choose your projects or dabble with your own innovations. Thus, you might consider minoring in business or going for your MBA. However, minoring in business would probably require an extra year as an undergraduate due to your already packed schedule.

If you love what you do and put your mind to the task without exception, you will continually awaken your senses on the road to a future beyond your expectations. Inventing next-generation products and staying on the cutting edge of technology helps humanity and provides the kind of fulfillment unavailable in

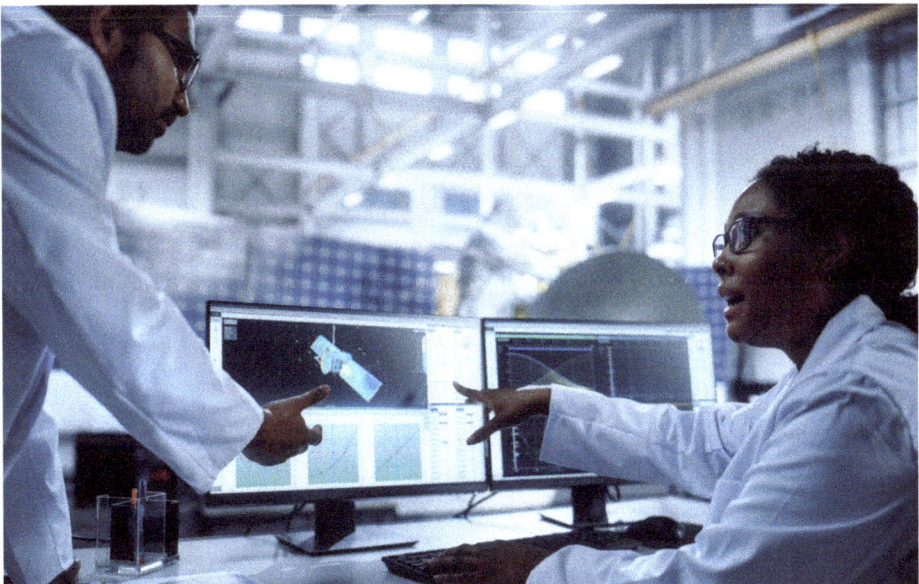

many careers. Moreover, autonomy and self-designed work offer freedom while also demanding discipline.

Some might say that the reality of Industrial Design work is quite different because working with others and the pressure of deadlines is far from stress-free. They are right. Disciplined effort requires numerous sacrifices. Besides, simultaneously mastering design, engineering, and business is not for the faint of heart. Still, for the fast-thinking, creatively-driven person, the rewards are worth the effort.

Your immersive college experience will expose you to the practices of great designers and the state-of-the-art alternative methodologies of contemporary idea-generators today. You will discover a wide range of options in each technology-infused class and determine your preferred styles and techniques. Professors, researchers, guest lecturers, and workshop hosts will help you continue to improve your skills while offering you feedback to go to the next level.

COMPELLING REASONS TO STUDY INDUSTRIAL DESIGN

1. Freedom of creative expression
2. Mind explosion of possibilities
3. Desire to draw, render, tell stories, and bring ideas to fruition
4. Love for experimentation with colors, forms, styles, shapes, and media
5. Interest in learning new technologies and computer software
6. Desire to work with a group toward a common goal
7. Hunger to create prototypes in a fast-paced, dynamic environment
8. Inquisitive desire to test, shape, mold, and adapt materials
9. Emotional feeling that beckons you toward engineering design
10. Opportunity to turn your passion for design into a lifetime career

In this constantly changing profession, which is continually upgrading and evolving, Industrial Designers must keep pace with rapid technology advancements. Today, socioeconomic and cultural influences offer new challenges as market forces adjust to what's hot and what's not. As a result, the ever-conscious, forward-thinking designer will need to think five paces ahead.

Amazing college professors who are successful in their own right will suggest ways for you to break into Industrial Design. A few faculty members who have outdated experiences, will not use the latest equipment or software since technology changes so rapidly. You might get frustrated. Don't. The fundamental principles of design and engineering will not change. Some college professors may even link you to their contacts for internships and jobs. Throughout college, you will discover your brand of professionalism along with a calling card of portfolio designs that allow others to understand what you offer.

"THERE IS NO ROYAL ROAD TO GEOMETRY" - EUCLID

When a student asked Euclid if there was an easier way to learn geometry, he cautioned that discipline and persistence are essential. Hard work is absolutely necessary. Additionally, there is no one way to succeed, just as there is no one way to design. You may choose to produce prototypes for a company, sell your inventions, teach science, or support other Industrial/Product Designers by sharing your wisdom.

Either way, engineering design is a versatile skill. Other professional options include engineering management, entertainment, education, and much more. You could manage a design firm or build a following through social media blogs. You might find that consulting is of interest or helping designers market their services is empowering.

Teaching is often considered a fallback. Yet, many teachers are inspired by the innocence and dreams of their students. Finally, management consulting pays extremely well. Firms like Bain, BCG, and McKinsey have excellent potential for bonuses and upward mobility. The hours are long, the work-life balance challenging, and you may frequently travel, but the projects are often fulfilling.

Thus, as you develop your skills, your talent is not wasted, not lost, not valueless. Instead, you can be a source of empowerment and strength for others.

TEACHING, EDUCATION, AND TRAINING

Kids clamor to create. Their imaginations run wild with ideas. Self-expression and exploration through design and engineering offer people young and old the chance to put their ideas onto a paper, computer, or still or moving medium. Lego projects, robotics, and scientific experiments offer limitless possibilities for the STEAM (Science, Technology, Engineering, Art, and Math) student.

As a result, there are numerous jobs in private and public education. Schools everywhere employ science and art teachers. Additionally, families hire science, engineering, and robotics coaches. Private studios conduct workshops and training. College professors can make more than $100,000/year teaching students while continuing to practice their craft. Of course, you would need to attend graduate school, but a master's degree in Industrial Design, Industrial Engineering, or Business would also take you to the next level of your profession. Furthermore, a doctorate opens new doors if you choose the research route. There is so much to innovate that you would never be bored.

In 2021, there were approximately 130,000 public and private K-12 schools in the United States, according to the National Center for Educational Statistics (NCES). During the 2020-2021 school year, there were 10,545 K-12 public schools and another 1,296 charter schools in California alone.[1] On the college level, during the 2019-2020 school year, there were 3,982 degree-granting higher education

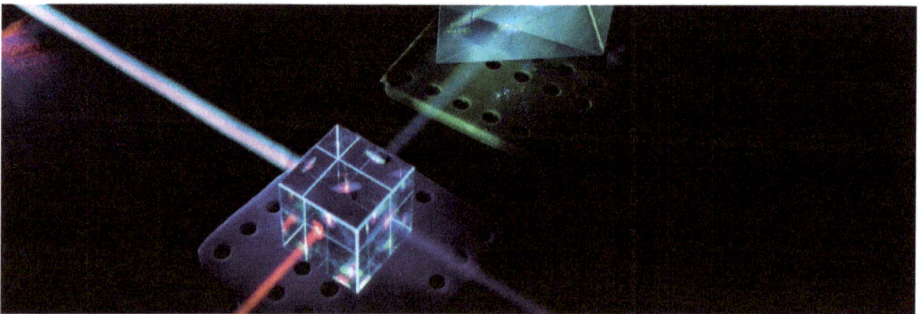

1 California Department of Education, "*Fingertip Facts on Education in California,*" 2020-2021, https://www.cde.ca.gov/ds/ad/ceffingertipfacts.asp

colleges and universities: 2,679 4-year and 1,303 2-year institutions.[2] Thus, there are numerous schools in which you may choose to work.

HARDWARE AND SOFTWARE SKILLS

You will spend much of your time on laptop computers and digitized machinery. The more you know, the better prepared you will be. A computer science class in high school or through a summer program would be extremely valuable. No doubt, computer programming, CAD design, graphic arts, or animation classes are a definite plus. Further, Industrial Design necessitates a strong foundation in computer graphics and technical drawing.

You are walking into a future where virtual reality and augmented reality will require greater technology skills than applicants had even ten years ago when most Industrial Designers created 2-D renderings that were often difficult to visualize. Yet, as you enter college, technology's rapid advancements will transform from primarily 2-D drawings to primarily 3-D virtual reality graphics.

A 3-D PRINTER IN EVERY SCHOOL

While 3-D printing machines were initially developed in the 1980s for rapid prototyping, the broader public got a glimpse of a desktop model by MakerBot, a company, that envisioned a 3-D printer in every home. Thousands of guests at the 2012 Consumer Electronics Show (CES) witnessed the creation of plastic parts created in front of them.

Nevertheless, what started as an expensive novelty machine changed its market focus when Stratasys purchased MakerBot and realigned its sales and distribution strategy toward the technology and education markets. Meanwhile, taking that idea to another level, designers created the human model machine where you stand inside a machine which casts a 3-D model of you. After CES, bright minds clamor to return home and create a better version of the most efficient and effective products. The show is three days of tantalizing inspiration for the maker in you.

Most college Industrial Design programs have access to 3-D printers in their fabrication spaces. At one point or another, while studying Industrial Design, 3-D printing will come into play. Projects are likely to include fabricating models,

---

2   NCES, "Digest of Education Statistics," U.S. Department of Education, 2020 Tables and Figures, https://nces. ed.gov/programs/digest/d20/tables/dt20_317.10.asp

handles, and parts. You may also be asked to design miniature cars, planes, or furniture using filament in a wide variety of colors with matte, silk, shiny, or transparent and finishes resembling wood, cardboard, and an assortment of metals. Some filaments even glow in the dark while others change color based upon temperature. Imagine the extraordinary possibilities.

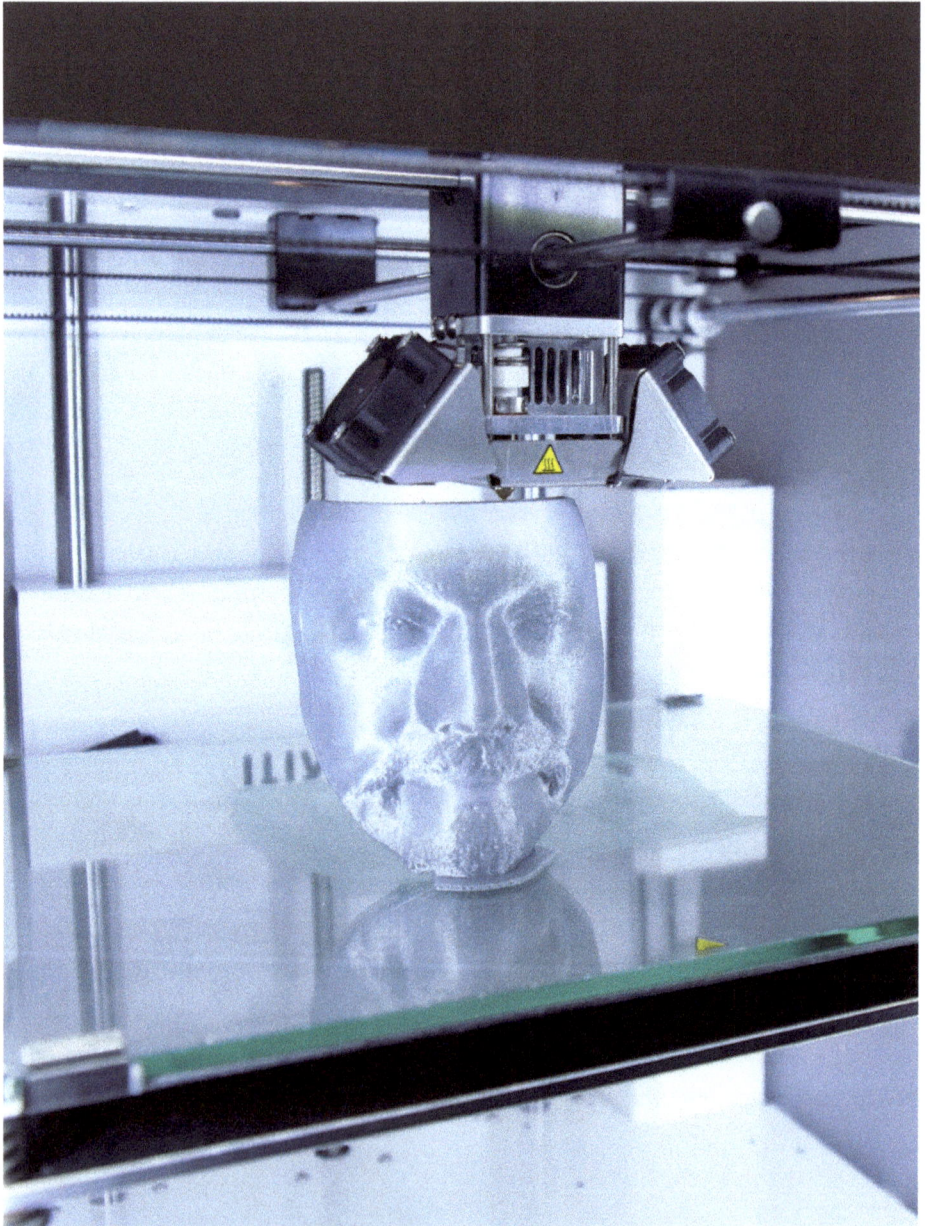

The point about 3-D printing, holograms, virtual reality, and augmented reality products is that any training you can do now in design, CAD, maker spaces, drawings, computer science, and digital arts will be extremely helpful. Find a location where you can experiment with these new technologies or volunteer in any capacity at an Industrial Design firm. Even if all you do is get coffee for people during your volunteer service, you will gain invaluable lessons as you watch how the firm ticks.

NEVER-ENDING FASCINATION

You will learn about history, consumerism, and society alongside creating eco-friendly products. Regional differences offer unique opportunities and challenges. Furthermore, overcoming legal restrictions can be a big factor in the success of a project. Securing materials, mitigating manufacturing factors, and working to obtain patents can be impediments or they can open new doors to partnerships. Experience makes a difference as young, brilliant, and eager neophytes seek to be recognized for their talents in a field where longevity, respect, and wisdom are often not acquired quickly.

The journey you are taking will have its ups and downs, but you will have stories to tell for the rest of your life. Your education may have unpredictable elements and pitfalls may lay in your path. Since you have endured a pandemic and the repercussions of a war, you are imbued with a few doses of resilience. Even so, you will be tested in architecture school as there is much to learn and a short amount of time.

You are embarking on a thrilling, demanding, and disciplined pursuit. You will work with extremely skilled and brilliant students who started studying science and mastered drawing complex images when they entered elementary school. Some who have worked in design firms will blow you away with their abilities. However, rarely are Industrial and Product Design students equally skilled in all areas. Some of your work will be a team effort where everyone will contribute what they know. You will too.

Some classmates will be amazingly talented. Do not let their abilities bring you down or make you feel as if you are not good enough. You will add your element and learn more during college. Besides, your enthusiasm for Industrial and Product Design will show through in your work and effort. Recognizing your potential, commitment, and attitude, people will be awed at your creations as you also step back to appreciate your work.

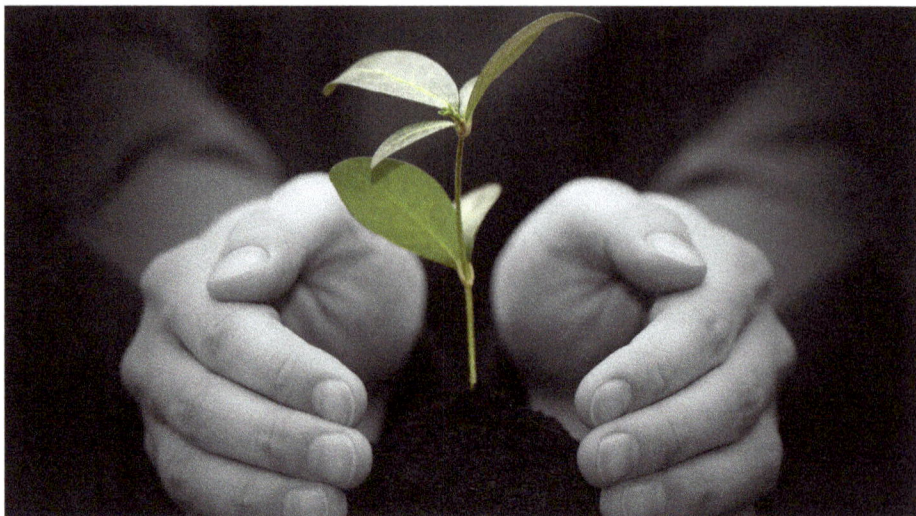

Enjoy the experience.

Don't judge each day by the harvest you reap but by the seeds that you plant.

- Robert Louis Stevenson

Even if the classes you want to take are not offered at your school, there are summer camps, short-term programs, online training, maker clubs, and college classes that would help you immensely along your way. Additional science classes would not hurt you at all either. Knowledge of chemistry and physics is imperative. The more you know, the more you will be able to access the information necessary to be a design guru.

Additionally, there is no way to understate the value of even a basic understanding of robotics. Building, programming, and working with robots in high school will help you while you are in college. Join or create a robotics team. See if there is a regional robotics club or league. If neither of these is available, find an avid robotics student and have them help you start from scratch.

Science unveils the mystery of the universe, and everything contained within can be explained by its principles. Thus, as you embark on your journey, learn as much as you can about science and mathematics. Remember that making a game plan now and challenging yourself to learn new and often difficult subjects is the first step along that journey.

Mathematics is the language in which God has written the universe.

- Galileo

LIMITLESS POSSIBILITIES

The preparation you receive will not restrict you. Even if one door is not open, knock on another one. Finding jobs can be frustrating, but a degree in Industrial Design is so versatile that there are dozens of directions you can go. You may find that your intended company or type of work does not pan out. One of my students changed fields to pursue video game design, which required an additional year of focused digital skills. However, he now leads a division in an amazing job that he truly enjoys.

The scope of design and engineering is expanding with new frontiers that offer opportunities never before imaginable. New industries and manufacturing facilities need designers to imagine and invent futuristic components. Furthermore, the Metaverse is an entirely new universe of possibilities. The ever-expanding need to innovate and improve products and systems is why some colleges have a half-dozen or more specialized majors in engineering, giving students the flexibility to double major and adapt their program with new areas of interest.

Studying Industrial Design will also keep you creative, allowing you to explore your evolving interests. The skills you learn in Industrial Design are fundamental to almost any field. Your options will be completely open, providing you with the freedom to choose. Industrial Design is increasingly recognized as a valuable skill. If you are passionate about this pursuit, one day, your efforts will bear fruit!

CHAPTER 5

SUMMER PROGRAMS & INTERNSHIPS FOR HIGH SCHOOL & COLLEGE STUDENTS

"Ambition is a dream with a V8 engine."

– Elvis Presley

S tart early to gain software, design, and engineering experiences. Internships and summer programs are as important in your educational pathway as coursework. The lessons you learn from working collaboratively and collegially with design-focused mentors is equally important. Historian and scholar, W.E.B. DuBois (1868-1963), a founding member of the NAACP and the first Black American to earn a Ph.D. at Harvard said, "Education must not simply teach work - it must teach life." Your college, experiential, and life education go hand-in-hand, driven by purpose and foresight since life truly is a journey, not a destination.

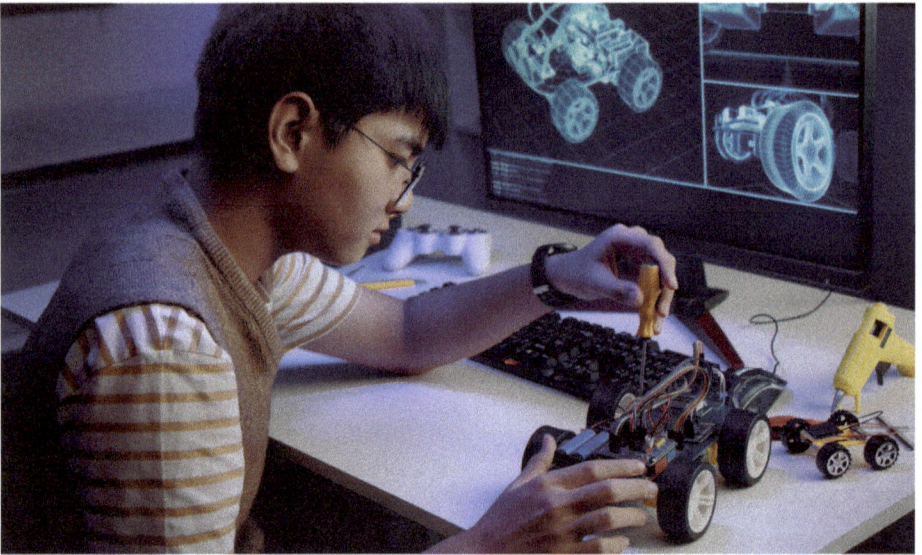

WHY PARTICIPATE IN SUMMER PROGRAMS/INTERNSHIPS?

You should participate in summer programs and internships. While some students and parents chose these options to look good and show dedication, the real reason why you should participate is to develop your skills with critique and feedback from specialists in the field. Discussions, seminars, studio work, and portfolio development are immensely valuable for your future pursuits. However, merely living on a campus and getting a feel for what college would be like cannot be understated.

Note: The following list is not exhaustive, and it is not an endorsement of any program. Dates, camps, internships, program descriptions, and program length may change from year to year.

SUMMER CAMPS & PROGRAMS FOR ART, DESIGN, FILM, PHOTOGRAPHY, AND ARCHITECTURE

Alabama

Auburn University – Architecture Camp – Creative Writing – Industrial Design

One week – Three Session Options – Full Scholarships Available (apply by April 1)
Students produce designs while working directly with professors.
Camp counselors support students with 24/7 questions, safety, and supervision.

Tuskegee University Taylor School of Architecture & Construction Science

Virtual Preview of Architecture and Construction at Tuskegee (V-PACT) 3-hour
Virtual Program. Preview Architecture & Construction Science 2-Week Program

Arizona

Arcosanti – Re-Imagined Urbanism – 6-week discussion-based classes - AZ

Combining architecture and ecology (arcology), you can learn in the World's First Prototype Arcology.

Core values: (1) Frugality and Resourcefulness, (2) Ecological Accountability, (3) Experiential Learning, and (4) Leaving a Limited Footprint, Arcosanti is juxtaposed to mass consumerism, urban sprawl, unchecked consumption, and social isolation.

National Institute of Health – 8-week Research Program – Phoenix, AZ

Research biomedical internship for students 17 years or older by June 15th.

Science and Engineering Apprenticeship Program (SEAP) – US Navy - Flagstaff

8-weeks, 300 openings, 30 laboratories nationwide, $4,000-$4,500 science and engineering research. High school students must be 16 years old or older. Apply starting in August for following summer.

Arkansas

University of Arkansas – In Person & Virtual Design Camp – Fayetteville, AK

In-Person Grades 9-12 - design projects, studio groups, tours, & meetings with local designers.

No fee; completely remote; design camp lessons embedded; students are paired with a faculty member in a studio group.

Advanced Design Camp: students entering Grades 11-12, 2 weeks in Fayetteville

California

Academy of Art Institute – San Francisco

4-6 weeks – Advertising, Animation/VFX, Architecture, Fashion, Fine Art, Game Development, Graphic Design.

Illustration, Industrial Design, Motion Pictures, Music Production, Photography, Writing for Film, TV, & Digital Media

Boeing Summer Internship – High School & College – Seal Beach & Palmdale, CA

Hands-on Industry Experience - Aviation and Engineering Internships

California State Summer School of the Arts (CSSSA) – Sacramento, CA

Rigorous 4-week, pre-professional visual and performing arts 2D and 3D training program in painting, printmaking, sculpture, ceramics, digital media, and photography; scholarship possibility for CA residents. Grades 9 – 12.

Canon Insights Summer Internship – Canon USA – Irvine, CA

Computer Science Major – 2nd or 3rd year; Position: Computer Vision Tech Assist with Quality Assurance Engineers; Digital Imaging Solution Division

COPE Scholars Program – Healthcare Internship – 280 Training/Experience Hrs

Locations: Anaheim/Orange, Bakersfield, Covina/Glendora, Hanford, Irvine, L.A., Mendocino County, Mission Viejo, Newport Beach, Oxnard, Riverside, Simi Valley, Tulare, Woodland Hills

Health Scholars must be 18+. Students assist w/basic healthcare for medical or nursing school, etc. Certificate of Completion - Keck Graduate Institute.

COSMOS – California State Summer School for Math & Science – 4 weeks; UC Campuses

Hands-on research program for California high school students (9-12) pursuing STEM fields; students live on campus and work with UC researchers. Application opens in January and closes in Feb. Topics from biomedical to space science.

Edwards Lifesciences Summer Internship Program – BS, MS, Ph.D., MBA - Irvine, CA

Currently Enrolled in College - Interested in Healthcare Related Programs
Proficient in Engineering Drafting Software, Writing, or Business/Leadership

Getty Museum – Paid Student Gallery Guide – Los Angeles, CA

Paid summer internship for teens ($2,400 in 2022). Learn the fundamentals of museums and public speaking while leading visitors around the grounds.

Also available – Open Call for teen photographers to share images, 8-week paid STEAM internship, and Summer Latin Academy at the Getty Villa to learn Latin.

Laguna College of Art & Design Pre-College Program – Laguna Beach, CA

Animation, Sculpture, Drawing Fundamentals, Figure Drawing, Graphic Design

NASA Jet Propulsion Laboratory – Pasadena, CA (Apply by March 31)

Paid Internship - Must be in an undergraduate in a STEM subject

Otis College of Art and Design Summer of Art – Los Angeles, CA

Intensive 4-week program for students 15+ for portfolio and studio training in architecture, conceptual art, digital media, graphic design, and printmaking, with lectures and critiques. Merit and need-based scholarships are available.

Parker Hannifin Corporation – Paid Summer Internship – Irvine, CA

Mechanical or Industrial Engineering Major – Flight Control, Aircraft Systems

Santa Clara University Summer Engineering Seminar (SES) – 10th and 11th Grade

4-day program introduces students to engineering practice, research, and education

School of Creative & Performing Arts (SOCAPA) – Occidental College (13-18-year-olds)

2-week, 3-week - learn Filmmaking, Screenwriting, Dance, Music, Photography

SCI-Arc (Southern California Institute of Architecture) Immersive 4-week Summer Program (Design Immersion Days) – Los Angeles

Introduction to the academic and professional world of architecture – Grades 9-12

Science and Engineering Apprenticeship Program (SEAP) – US Navy Camp Pendleton, Port Hueneme, Pt. Mugu, San Diego, Monterey, Corona

8-weeks, 300 openings, 30 laboratories nationwide, $4,000-$4,500 science and engineering research. High school students must be 16 years old or older. Apply starting in August for following summer.

SpaceX – Summer Engineering/Co-op Program – Locations in

Hawthorne, Irvine, and Vandenberg AFB
Paid Internship - Must be an undergraduate in a STEM subject

Stanford Programs - SUMaC – Stanford University Mathematics Camp; Humanities Institute; Stanford Institutes of Medicine Research Program

10th and 11th Grade – Highly competitive 3-week programs for exceptional students with proven subject mastery; Application Deadline: March 15.

Stanford University – 8-Week Summer Courses and 3-Week Arts Institute

Architecture, Art, Drawing, Dance, Creative Writing, Music, and Photography

Tesla Internships – Average $33/hour – Dozens of Positions Throughout CA

Full-Time Automotive Design, Engineering Technologies, Vehicle Service Research/Training

UCLA Summer Jumpstart Summer Art Inst, Digital Media Arts Inst., Digital Filmmaking Institute, and Game Lab Institute

2-week program - Portfolio development– credit available
Drawing, Painting, Photography, Sculpture, Video Art, Animation, and Game Design

USC Summer Film, Writing, and Architecture Programs – Los Angeles

2-4-week program, "Creative Writing Workshop", "Comedy Performance", "Exploration into Architecture"

Colorado

National Security Agency (NSA) – Paid Computer Internship – Aurora

Students must be at least a junior in high school with interest in business, engineering, or computer science. Apply between September 1 and October 31.

Connecticut

Science and Engineering Apprenticeship Program (SEAP) – US Navy – Groton

8-weeks, 300 openings, 30 laboratories nationwide, $4,000-$4,500 science and engineering research. High school students must be 16 years old or older. Apply starting in August for following summer.

Summer Studio: Discovering Graphic Design (AIGA) – Bridgeport, CT

Free 4-week hands-on program for Bridgeport rising juniors and seniors
Week 1 – Music Festival Poster, Week 2 – Digital Media Poster
Week 3 – Animating Your Ideas, Week 4 – Portfolio Art for College Applications

District of Columbia

Catholic University School of Architecture and Planning

Summer High School Program - 2-week Residential (Two Session Options)

George Washington University Digital Storytelling Pre-College Program – July

Produce stories with smartphones, learn storyboarding, and broadcast through social media; craft ideas, capture images, & create compelling content, including character development.

Georgetown University – 1-week – Creative Writing – Publishing

Fiction, Short Story, Poetry, and Professional Writing; visit literary hubs

National Air and Space Museum in Washington, D.C. – HS and College Students

The Explainers Program offers a 15 hr/month year round paid position for students to help visitors better understand the Museum and its artifacts and exhibitions.

Florida

Florida Atlantic University – Boca Raton, FL and Ft. Lauderdale, FL

School of Architecture – July (Three Session Options)

July 3-week program for rising sophomores, juniors, seniors, and students in their first 2 years of college - Portfolio development, fabrication, architectural education, portfolio display, critique

Certificate of Completion Awarded – Enrollment on a first-come, first-served basis

Ringling College of Art and Design – Sarasota, FL

Intensive 4-week program focused on art and design including computer animation, creative writing, digital sculpting, entertainment design, fabrication, film directing/production, game art, game design, illustration, painting, photography, storyboarding, and virtual reality development.

Science and Engineering Apprenticeship Program (SEAP) – US Navy
Patrick SFB, Jacksonville, Orlando, Panama City

8-weeks, 300 openings, 30 laboratories nationwide, $4,000-$4,500 science and engineering research. High school students must be 16 years old or older. Apply starting in August for following summer.

SpaceX – Summer Engineering/Co-op Program – Cape Canaveral, FL

Paid Internship - Must be in an undergraduate in a STEM subject

University of Florida Design Exploration Program (DEP)

3-week Residential Immersion into the architectural studio environment. Construction of studio design projects, teamwork, seminars, field trips, architectural theory.

University of Miami Summer Scholars, Explorations in Architecture & Design– Coral Gables, FL

3-week Residential program; 6 college credits; Design, Graphics, and Theory. Architecture, Landscape Architecture, Historic Preservation; Urban Planning. Studio experience with drawing, model making, drafting, CAD, visual analysis.

Georgia

Emory University – Atlanta, GA – 2-, 4-, 6-Week Writing Programs

Journalism, Dramatic Writing, Media & Politics, Psychology & Fiction

Georgia Institute of Technology Pre-College Design Program – Atlanta, GA

2-week Residential program – College of Design – Grades 11 & 12 (Two Session Options); Architecture, Building Construction, Industrial Design, and Music Technology

National Security Agency (NSA) – Paid Computer Internship – Augusta

Students must be at least a junior in high school with interest in business, engineering, or computer science. Apply between September 1 and October 31.

Savannah College of Art & Design – Savannah, GA - SCAD 5-week Rising Star & SCAD courses

2-week College of Design Residential program –– Grades 11 & 12 - Courses include Advertising, Animation, Virtual Reality, Illustration, Storyboarding, Photography, Painting, Fashion, Digital Film, Graphic Design, and Industrial Design

Hawaii

COPE Scholars Program – Healthcare Internship – 280 Hrs Training/Experience Location in Kailua

Health Scholars must be 18+. Students assist w/basic healthcare for medical or nursing school, etc. Certificate of Completion - Keck Graduate Institute.

National Security Agency (NSA) – Paid Computer Internship – Oahu

Students must be at least a junior in high school with interest in business, engineering, or computer science. Apply between September 1 and October 31.

Science and Engineering Apprenticeship Program (SEAP) – US Navy – Honolulu

8-weeks, 300 openings, 30 laboratories nationwide, $4,000-$4,500 science and engineering research. High school students must be 16 years old or older. Apply starting in August for following summer.

Illinois

Illinois Institute of Technology Summer Introduction to Architecture

2-week Experiment in Architecture for HS students – Comprehensive overview 1-week Exploration in Architecture for middle school students – studio-based, firm visits, field trips, projects.

Northwestern University – National HS Institute

5-week Film & Video, Music, Speech & Debate, Theatre

School of the Art Institute of Chicago – Early College Program for HS Students

1-, 2-, 4-week Residential programs in Painting, Drawing, Animation, Comics/ Graphic Novels, and Fashion Design.

Portfolio development programs; earn college credit. Full-tuition scholarships are available.

Southern Illinois University Carbondale – Kid Architecture

1-week Elementary Grades, Middle School & High School Architecture Camp

University of Illinois at Chicago Architecture - HiArch Summer High School Program

1-, 2-week (July) - HS students are introduced to the culture of architecture, design, thinking, and making.

University of Chicago Creative Writing Immersion

"Collegiate Writing: Awakening Into Consciousness" and "Creative Writing: Fiction"

Indiana

Science and Engineering Apprenticeship Program (SEAP) – US Navy – Crane

8-weeks, 300 openings, 30 laboratories nationwide, $4,000-$4,500 science and engineering research. High school students must be 16 years old or older. Apply starting in August for following summer.

University of Notre Dame Summer Scholars Program

2-weeks HS Students – Film, Photography, Performing Arts - studios, seminars, and field trips

Iowa

Iowa State University – College of Design - HS Design Camps

1-week HS Students – Architecture, Studio/Fine Arts, Graphic Design, Interior Design, & Industrial Design

Louisiana

Science and Engineering Apprenticeship Program (SEAP) – US Navy – New Orleans

8-weeks, 300 openings, 30 laboratories nationwide, $4,000-$4,500 science and engineering research. High school students must be 16 years old or older. Apply starting in August for following summer.

Maryland

Goddard Space Flight Center (NASA) - High School & College

Summer Internship - Greenbelt, MD
Research, Mentorship, Experiential Learning Opportunities

Maryland Institute College of Art (MICA) – Baltimore, MD

2-, 3-, 5-week HS Students – Live instruction, studio time, workshops, artist talks, collaboration, feedback, critique, evaluation

National Institute of Health – 8-week – Bethesda

Research biomedical internship for students 17 years or older by June 15th.

National Security Agency (NSA) – Paid Computer Internship – Ft. Meade

Students must be at least a junior in high school with interest in business, engineering, or computer science. Apply between September 1 and October 31.

Science and Engineering Apprenticeship Program (SEAP) – US Navy – Bethesda, Patuxent River, Silver Spring, Indian Head, and Annapolis

8-weeks, 300 openings, 30 laboratories nationwide, $4,000-$4,500 science and engineering research. High school students must be 16 years old or older. Apply starting in August for following summer.

University of Maryland – 4-week ESTEEM/SER-Quest Summer Program

Rising seniors undertake engineering-focused projects while conducting research

Massachusetts

Boston College - Boston, MA – Creative Writing Seminar Program

3-week (July) Residential Program – HS Students – nonfiction, fiction, poetry Create & edit the class literary journal and present writings at a public reading

Boston University Math, Engineering, Technology, Media, and Journalism

AMP - Academy of Media Production – Cinematic/journalistic in visual storytelling (Grades 10 – 12)

Code Breakers – 10th and 11th Grade Females - Cybersecurity, Cryptography, Programming (Free)

GirlsGetMath@BU – 5-day Non-residential summer program for enthusiastic 10th – 11th graders

Journalism Academy – 2-week Training in Writing, Photography, Reporting (students 14-18)

PROMYS – **Program in Mathematics for Young Scientists** – 6 weeks 80 high school students 14+ years old (scholarships available); seminars in number theory, cryptography, linear algebra, matroids, graphs, and data visualization.

RISE – **Research in Science & Engineering** - 6-week Research in Science & Engineering program in astronomy, chemistry, neuroscience, and medicine. Engineering Research Options: Biomedical, Computer, Electrical, Mechanical

U-Design – 2-week Engineering Design Program – hands-on build workshop (Grades 6 – 10)

Harvard University GSD Design Discovery– Cambridge, MA (Ages 18-mid-career professionals)

3-week Residential Program – Architecture, Landscape, Urban Planning & Design Physical modeling, fabrication, assembly

Harvard Summer Program for High School Students

2-week non-credit program; 7-week college credit program (live in campus dorms)

Credit classes include: Creating Comics & Graphic Novels; Drawing & the Digital Age; Advertising, Landscape, & Visual Imagery; Creative Writing

Massachusetts College of Art & Design – 4-Week Art Immersion Program

Students take 3 foundation courses; closing exhibition

Massachusetts Institute of Technology – HS Students – Cambridge

Urbanframe Summer Design - Build Project CAD, drafting, sketching, mapping and context study, historical research, carpentry & construction

MITES – Minority Introduction to Engineering and Science – Intensive 6-week residential program for 80 high school juniors who intend to enter STEM programs, especially from underrepresented groups. The program is free.

RSI – Research Science Institute – Intensive 6-week program for 70 high school juniors who study advanced theory/research in math, science, and engineering. The program is free.

WTP – Women's Technology Program – 4-week engineering program focused on EE, ME, or EECS.

SSP – Summer Science Program – Research program on Astrophysics or Biochemistry. This 6-week research program is located in Colorado, New Mexico, and Indiana.

Beaver Works Summer Institute – 4-week intensive program for first-generation high school juniors. Programs include Autonomous Underwater Vehicles to Quantum Software and to Serious Game Design with AI.

Additional MIT Hosted Programs: LaunchX, LLRise (Lincoln Laboratory Radar), OSC, iD Tech Camps, National Geographic Student Expeditions

National Institute of Health – 8-week – Framingham

Research biomedical internship for students 17 years or older by June 15th.

Tufts University – 6-Week Writing Intensive

Writing exercises, evaluation from professors, revise, develop papers that build on a theme

University of Massachusetts Amherst Pre-College – Amherst, MA

1-, 2-, 3-week Residential Intensives Grades 10-12; 3-D Design, 3-D Animation, Building & Construction Technology; Combatting the Climate Crisis Summer Engineering Institute, Design Academy, Programming for Aspiring Scientists

Wellesley College – Wellesley, MA

2-week Residential Program - EXPLO Pre-College + Career for Grades 10-12 Three session options; Topics include – AI, Entrepreneurship, Engineering, Medicine, Law, CSI

Youth Design Boston (AIGA) – Boston, MA

Summer Graphic Design Internship & Mentoring Program

Michigan

Andrews University School of Architecture & Interior Design - Renaissance Kids – Berrien Springs, MI

Virtual Studio Projects; lecture; community build projects

Interlochen Center for the Arts – Summer Arts Camp – 1-6 Weeks

Creative Writing, Dance, Art, Motion Picture, Music, Theatre, Visual Arts

National Institute of Health – 8-week – Detroit

Research biomedical internship for students 17 years or older by June 15th.

University of Michigan – Stamps School of Art & Design – BFA Preview

3-week (June/July)– HS Students – Creative retreat with state-of-the-art facilities & museum excursions

University of Michigan – Summer Engineering Exploration Camp (SEE)

1-week, co-ed, residential program resolving engineering design challenges Apply Jan-Feb – Grades 10-12

Mississippi

Science and Engineering Apprenticeship Program (SEAP) – US Navy – Stennis

8-weeks, 300 openings, 30 laboratories nationwide, $4,000-$4,500 science and engineering research. High school students must be 16 years old or older. Apply starting in August for following summer.

Missouri

Washington University in St. Louis – Creative Writing Institute and HS Summer Scholars Program

2-week program – fiction, nonfiction, and poetry; morning writer's workshops – editing and sharing work
5-8 week – Dance, Journalism, Photography, Music, Drama, Photojournalism

University of Missouri Kansas City – Department of Architecture, Urban Planning & Design MA

Design Discovery Program – Architecture, Interior Design, Landscape Architecture
3-day (July) Non-Residential Program – HS Students/Current College Students

Nebraska

University of Nebraska College of Architecture – Lincoln, NE

6-day (June) Residential Program – Grades 11 & 12 – Studio training; architectural design; scholarships

New Jersey

New Jersey Institute of Technology – Hillier College of Architecture & Design

1-week (July) Residential Program – HS Students – Architecture, Interior Design, Industrial Design, Digital Design
Summer Architecture + Design Programs (2 Start Dates)

Science and Engineering Apprenticeship Program (SEAP) – US Navy – Lakehurst

8-weeks, 300 openings, 30 laboratories nationwide, $4,000-$4,500 science and engineering research. High school students must be 16 years old or older. Apply starting in August for following summer.

New York

AIA New York – Center for Architecture

1-week (July) Residential Program – HS Students – Architecture
Programs for Grades 3-12 include Architectural Design Studio, Drawing Architecture, Rooftop Dwelling, Dream House, Treehouses, Skyscrapers, Green Island Home, Subway Architecture, Waterfront City, Parks & Playground Design, and Neighborhood Design

Canon Insights Summer Internship – Canon USA – PR/Marketing - Huntington, NY

Public Relations & Marketing Majors – 10 Week Paid Position

Columbia University - New York, NY – Summer Immersion

3-week July-August Residential Program – Architecture, Creative Writing, Drawing, Filmmaking, Photography, Theater, or Visual Arts

Cooper Union - New York, NY – Summer Art Intensive

4-week July-August Residential Programs – Portfolio Development, Exhibition, Anthology Publication; Animation, Creative Writing, Photography, Drawing, Graphic Design, & Stop Animation

Cornell University – Ithaca, NY – Precollege Studies and 3-Week Transmedia: Image, Sound, Motion Program

3-, 6-, 9-week June-August Residential Program; Drawing and New Media (collage, drawing, digital photography, screen printing, & video)
Architecture: Design Studio, Culture, and Society, Architectural Science & Technology

Cornell University – CURIE Academy for Females going into 11th and 12th

Students who excel in math and science *break the rules* to make new discoveries.

Corning Summer Internships for College Students – Corning, NY

Advanced Optics, Gorilla Glass, Emerging Innovations, Life Sciences, Pharmaceuticals Internships Offered in Engineering, Science, and Business

Goddard Institute for Space Studies Summer Internship - High School & College

Research, Mentorship, and Experiential Learning Opportunities

Jacobs Institute 8-week Paid Biomedical Internship (Apply Nov.-Jan.)

HS Jr/Sr or Enrolled College Student – Gates Vascular Institute, Buffalo Niagara Medical Campus; Lunch and Learn, Weekly Grand Rounds, Research, Presentations

New York University Summer Art Intensive

4-week Immersive program in Digital & Video, Sculpture, or Visual Arts

New York University Applied Research in Science and Engineering

ARISE is a Free 7-week STEM program focused on Biomedical, Chemical Civil, Computer, Electrical, Mechanical, and Aerospace Engineering

Parsons School of Design – New York and Paris

4-week - Online and on-campus summer programs for students from 3rd grade to 12th NYC - Portfolio building in 3-credit immersive Design, Studio Art, Photography, Illustration, Game Design
Paris Program – Design & Mgmt, Explorations in Drawing & Painting, Fashion Design

Rensselaer Polytechnic University – Troy, NY

Architecture Career Discovery Program

School of Creative & Performing Arts (SOCAPA) – New York (13-18-year-olds)

2-, 3-week - Learn Filmmaking, Screenwriting, Dance, Music, Photography

Sotheby's Summer Institute – Pre-College, Undergrad, Graduate, and Professional

New York, London, and Virtual Programs; Intensives in Painting & Drawing, Curating, Luxury Marketing, Art Crime/Art Law, Fashion, and Art Business

Spotify – Summer Internship with The Journal – New York (Remote Eligible)

Research, Writing, News Stories, Podcast Work
Partnership between Gimlet and the Wall Street Journal

Syracuse University – Syracuse, NY – On-Campus and Online Programs for HS Students

2-, 3-, 6-week programs 3-D Studio Art; Sculpture; Architecture; Design Studies; Writing Immersion

North Carolina

Corning Summer Internships for College Students – NW Charlotte, NC

Advanced Optics, Gorilla Glass, Emerging Innovations, Life Sciences, Pharmaceuticals Internships Offered in Engineering, Science, and Business

National Institute of Health – 8-week – Research Triangle Park

Research biomedical internship for students 17 years or older by June 15th.

Science and Engineering Apprenticeship Program (SEAP) – US Navy – Cherry Point

8-weeks, 300 openings, 30 laboratories nationwide, $4,000-$4,500 science and engineering research. High school students must be 16 years old or older. Apply starting in August for following summer.

Ohio

Science and Engineering Apprenticeship Program (SEAP) – US Navy – Dayton

8-weeks, 300 openings, 30 laboratories nationwide, $4,000-$4,500 science and engineering research. High school students must be 16 years old or older. Apply starting in August for following summer.

Oklahoma

University of Oklahoma Architecture Summer Academy

1-week (June) Residential Program – HS Students – Architecture, Interior Design, Construction Science Design in Action: Creativity, Innovation, and Sustainability Shaping the Built Environment

Pennsylvania

Carnegie Mellon University Pre-College Art Program - Pittsburgh, PA

3-, 4-, 6-week (July-August) Residential Program – Intensive Studio Studies Portfolio development in Drawing, Sculpture, Animation, and Concept Studio Art Chestnut Hill College Global Solutions Lab

Carnegie Mellon Summer Academy for Math & Science - Pittsburgh

Free. STEM opportunity for students from underrepresented communities to explore science with hands-on projects and classroom instruction.

Interactive Global Simulation, Electrifying Africa, & UN Sustainable Development Goals

1-week programs – HS Students – Intensive collaborative team solutions to big problems

Drexel University Westphal College of Media Arts & Design – Discovering Architecture

2-week Residential Program – HS Students – Intensive Studio Architecture Program Visit prominent architectural, multi-disciplinary design offices; meet architects

Maywood University Pre-College Summer Workshop School of Architecture

2-week (July) Residential Program – HS Students – Design Your Future Architecture Program

Pennsylvania State University Architecture & Landscape Architecture Summer Camp

1-week (July) – HS Students –Architecture, Graphics, Design, and the Built Environment Program

Science and Engineering Apprenticeship Program (SEAP) – US Navy – Philadelphia

8-weeks, 300 openings, 30 laboratories nationwide, $4,000-$4,500 science and engineering research. High school students must be 16 years old or older. Apply starting in August for following summer.

Temple University Tyler School of Art and Architecture Pre-College Program

2-week (July-August) Residential Program – HS Students – Studio Architecture

Rhode Island

Brown University – 1-4 Weeks – Art Themed Courses

Creative Writing, Music, Studio Art, Art History

Rhode Island School of Design Pre-College School of Design – Providence, RI

6-week (June-July) Residential Program – HS Students – Foundational Art & Design Studies Figure drawing, projects, trips, exhibitions

Roger Williams University High School Summer Academy in Architecture

4-week (July-August) Residential Program – Grades 11 & 12 – Explore Studio Architecture - Seminars, fieldwork, studio, portfolio development

South Carolina

Clemson University Pre-College School of Architecture Program

1-week (July-August) Residential Program – Grades 7-12 - Engineering Design, Mechanical/Civil Engineering, Intelligent Vehicles, Materials Engineering

Science and Engineering Apprenticeship Program – US Navy – Charleston

8-weeks, 300 openings, 30 laboratories nationwide, $4,000-$4,500 science and engineering research. High school students must be 16 years old or older. Apply starting in August for following summer.

Tennessee

The University of Memphis Discovering Architecture + Design

1-day – HS Students – Design programs on architecture, interior design, and the built environment

The University of Tennessee, Knoxville College of Architecture + Design

1-week UT Summer Design Camp (July) Residential – HS Students Immersive architecture, graphic design, and professional practice program

Vanderbilt Summer Academy – Nashville, TN – 3-Week Program

"Digital Storytelling", "Writing Fantasy Fiction", "Math & Music", "Writing Short Stories"

Texas

Boeing Summer Internship – HS & College– Lewisville and San Antonio

Hands-on Industry Experience - Aviation and Engineering Internships

Corning Summer Internships for College Students – Keller, TX

Advanced Optics, Gorilla Glass, Emerging Innovations, Life Sciences, Pharmaceuticals Internships Offered in Engineering, Science, and Business

Jacobs Engineering Internship – Summer Internship (College) - Dallas

Civil, Electrical, Environmental, Geotechnical, & Transportation Engineering;

Sustainability, Cybersecurity, Mobility, and R&D with worldwide projects.

National Security Agency (NSA) – Paid Computer Internship – San Antonio

Students must be at least a junior in high school with interest in business, engineering, or computer science. Apply between September 1 and October 31.

SpaceX – Summer Engineering/Co-op Program – Brownsville and McGregor, TX

Paid Internship - Must be in an undergraduate in a STEM subject

Tesla Internships – Ave. $33/hour – Full-Time Automotive Design/ Engineering

Austin – Manufacturing Engineering; Waco - People Analytics - Vehicle Service Research/Training

Texas Tech Anson L Clark Scholars Program – Research Areas: Advertising, Architecture, Art, Dance, Engineering, or Theatre

7-week – Grades 11 & 12 – Residential Program (must be 17 years old by start date) – no program fee

Intensive research-based program; $500 meal card; $750 tax-free stipend

University of Texas at Austin - My Introduction to Engineering (MITE)

5-day camp for 11th grade students to work on team-based engineering projects

University of Houston & Wonderworks Pre-College Summer Discovery Program

Hines College of Architecture & Design – Introduction to Architecture

6-week – HS Students – Design programs with hands-on studio, field trips, and portfolio workshop

The University of Texas at Austin Summer Design Camps – 2-D Game Design, 3-D Game Design, 3-D Animation/Motion

School of Design and Creative Technologies
1-week – HS Students – portfolio development and design

Utah

Edwards Lifesciences Summer Internship Program – BS, MS, Ph.D., MBA - Draper, Utah

Currently Enrolled in College - Interested in Healthcare Related Programs
Proficient in Engineering Drafting Software, Writing, or Business/Leadership

Vermont

School of Creative & Performing Arts (SOCAPA) – Burlington, VT (13-18-year-olds)

2-week, 3-week - learn Filmmaking, Screenwriting, Dance, Music, Photography

Virginia

NASA's Wallops Flight Facility Summer Internship - High School & College

Research, Mentorship, and Experiential Learning Opportunities

Northrop Grumman – Engineering Intern– Space Systems R & D Team

Graduating HS Seniors – Join an engineering team to design, develop and test space systems and satellites; R & D - land, sea, air, space, and cyberspace.

Science and Engineering Apprenticeship Program (SEAP) – US Navy Hampton Roads and Dahlgren

8-weeks, 300 openings, 30 laboratories nationwide, $4,000-$4,500 science and engineering research. High school students must be 16 years old or older. Apply starting in August for following summer.

Virginia Commonwealth University (VCUArts) Pre-College

3-Week On-Campus Program Course Options – 2D Portfolio Development, Photography; Clay: More Than Just Mud, Sketchbook to Controller, Animation Workshop, Sculptural Forms, Jewelry Making, Fashion Design, Stage Combat, Musical Theatre, Acting From Page to Stage

Virginia Tech Inside Architecture + Design

1-week – HS Students – Hands-on design studio architecture program

Washington

COPE Scholars Program – Healthcare Internship – 280 Hours Training Locations in Puyallup, Seattle, Spokane, and Tacoma

Health Scholars must be 18+. Students assist w/basic healthcare for medical or nursing school, etc. Certificate of Completion - Keck Graduate Institute.

DigiPen Academy – K-12 Animation, Film, Music, Game Design Summer Programs – Redmond, WA

1-week and 2-week programs, including Teen Art & Animation; Film Scoring Music & Sound Design; Video Game Development; Animation Masterclass

Science and Engineering Apprenticeship Program (SEAP) – US Navy – 2 WA Locations

8-weeks, 300 openings, 30 laboratories nationwide, $4,000-$4,500 science and engineering research. High school students must be 16 years old or older. Apply starting in August for following summer.

University of Washington – Seattle, WA – Middle and HS Students

1-Week - Neurotechnology Young Scholars Program, DawgBytes Computer Science Camp, Material Science Camp, and Summer Session Art Classes

West Virginia

NASA Independent Verification and Validation Facility, Fairmont, WV

Research, Mentorship, and Experiential Learning Opportunities

Wisconsin

The University of Wisconsin Milwaukee School of Architecture & Urban Planning

1-week – HS Students – Design program on architecture, interior design, and the built environment

TAKE ADVANTAGE OF THIS TIME TO EXPLORE

During high school and college, you have the opportunity to explore your interests through summer programs, skill-building camps, and internships. Try out different fields you might not have considered before. You never really have the same chance to consider alternatives in quite the same way. Learn something new. There are hundreds of career areas you may never have considered. Have some fun while you are at it!

Everything has its beauty, but not everyone sees it.

– Andy Warhol

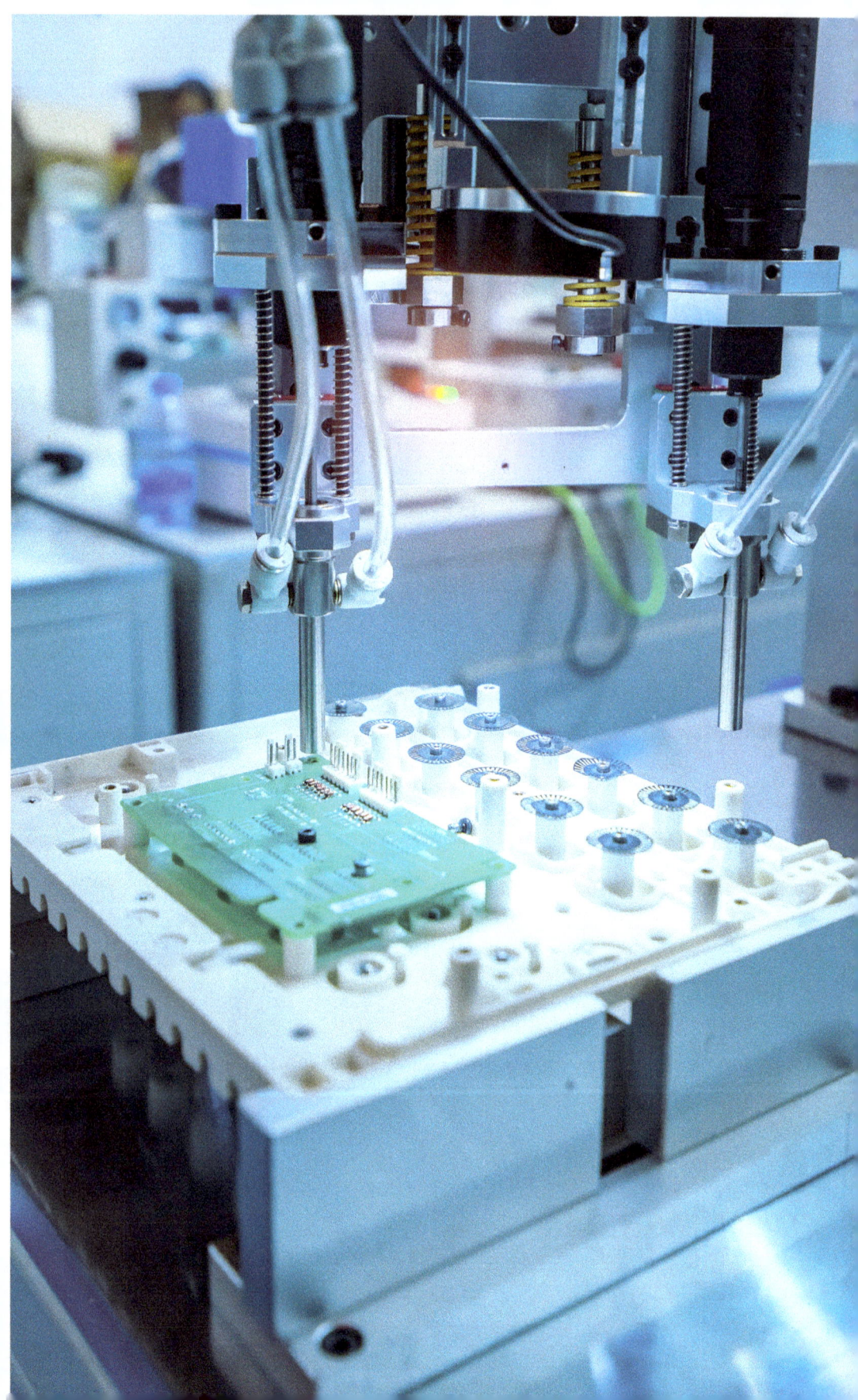

CHAPTER 6

UNIVERSITY OPTIONS: COLLEGE PROGRAMS FOR INDUSTRIAL & PRODUCT DESIGN

"There's no such thing in anyone's life as an unimportant day."

– Alexander Woollcott

I n the United States, 42 universities offer an industrial design degree. According to IBISWorld, an industry research firm, 29,536 people were employed in 2022 as Industrial Designers in the United States. Additionally, there were 15,088 Industrial Design firms in the United States. The pandemic caused a drop in employment, which is now steadily increasing at 6.1% in annualized market size growth as more products are being envisioned, developed, and manufactured.

By the numbers, here are some big picture data for 2022.

19.6 million U.S. College Students

14.5 million attending public colleges

5.14 million attending private colleges

2,679 4-year colleges

1,303 2-year colleges

Another interesting statistic is that undergraduate enrollment dropped more than 4% from fall 2019 to fall 2020 and another 3.5% from fall 2020 to fall 2021, representing approximately a 1,500,000 loss of students during the pandemic. However, with test-optional admissions opening the door to more students without test scores or who test poorly, more students applied to the top schools.

INDUSTRIAL DESIGNERS SOCIETY OF AMERICA (IDSA) (2022 MEMBER COLLEGES)

Academy of Art University

Auburn University

Carnegie Mellon University – Integrated Innovation Institute

University of Pennsylvania – Integrated Product Design

Kean University – Michael Graves College

Paier College

Rochester Institute of Technology – College of Art and Design ID

San Francisco State – School of Design

Cedarville University – International Center for Creativity

Philadelphia University/Thomas Jefferson University

University of Cincinnati

University of Oregon – Department of Product Design

USC Iovine and Young Academy

ADMISSIONS DATA TO CONSIDER

University	Total # Applied	Total Admit Rate	# Applied Regular Decision	# of Admits Regular	Reg. Dec. Admit Rate	Applied ED/SEA	Accepted Early Dec or SEA	ED/SEA Admit Rate
Brown	50,649	5.03%	44,503	1,651	3.71%	6,146	896	14.58%
Columbia	60,377	3.73%	54,072	1,603	2.96%	6,305	650	10.31%
Cornell	71,000	10.3%	61,500	3,922	6.7%	9,500	1,930	21.4%
Dartmouth	28,336	6.2%	25,703	1,237	4.81%	2,633	530	20.13%
Harvard	61,220	3.19%	51,814	1,214	2.34%	9,406	740	7.87%
Penn	55,000	4.4%	47,205	2,008	4.2%	7,795	1.218	15.63%
Princeton		3.98%	Princeton did not publish data for 2025 & will not publish data for 2026					
Yale	50,015	4.46%	42,727	1,434	3.36%	7,288	800	10.98%

University	Total # Applied	Total Admit Rate	Applied ED/Early Action	Accepted ED/Early Action	ED/EA Admit Rate
Boston College	40,477	16.5%	4,443	1,250	28.13%
Boston U	80,792	14.15%	6,311	1,640	25.99%
Duke	50,002	6.17%	4,015	855	21.3%
Emory	33,559	10.66%	2,127	672	31.59%
Georgetown	26,670	12.11%	8,832	881	9.98%
GWU	27,301	49%	1051	681	65%
Georgia Tech	50,601	17.14%	6,100	2,399	39.33%
Harvey Mudd	4,440	12.97%	Unavailable		
Johns Hopkins	37,100	6.49%	2,500	520	20.8%
MIT	33,976	3.94%	14,781	697	4.72%
NYU	105,000	12.2%	19,000	7,220	38%
Northeastern ED	91,100	6.7%	2,700	880	32.59%
Northeastern EA			50,000	3,000	6%
Northwestern	51,554	7.0%	26,506	1,675	12.87%
Notre Dame	26,506	12.87%	9,683	1,675	17.30%
Rice	31,424	8.56%	2,700	650	24.07%
Tufts	34,880	9.0%	Unavailable		
Tulane	42,000	10.0%	26,483	4,588	17.32%
USC	69,000	11.88%	USC does not have EA, ED, or REA		
Vanderbilt	46,717	6.13%	2,700	650	24.07%
Villanova	23,813	23.%	2025 – EA - 25.2%, ED – 58%		
Wash U St. L.	35,980	10.0%	Unavailable		17.6%
Wesleyan	14,521	13.86%	2026 – EDI - 44%, EDII – 31%		

UNIVERSITY OF CALIFORNIA

The 2022 University of California Fact Sheet data below from UC Admissions, says, "Data are Subject to Change". Nonetheless, here is a comparison between admissions to the class of 2024 and admission to the class of 2026.

UNIVERSITY OF CALIFORNIA ADMISSIONS DATA				
University of California Campus	Residency of Applicants	Number of Applications		Acceptance Rate Class of 2026
		Class of 2024	Class of 2026	
Berkeley	California	50,223	72,417	14.5%
	Out-of-State	20,659	32,580	
	International	17,114	23,195	
	Total	88,026	128,192	
Davis	California	54,570	65,367	49.0%
	Out-of-State	6,505	10,748	
	International	15,798	18,610	
	Total	76,873	94,725	
Irvine	California	72,391	84,743	29.0%
	Out-of-State	8,000	14,309	
	International	17,525	20,113	
	Total	97,916	119,165	
Los Angeles	California	67,877	91,544	10.8%
	Out-of-State	23,016	34,627	
	International	17,944	23,608	
	Total	108,837	149,779	
Merced	California	22,244	22,516	87.6%
	Out-of-State	598	1,319	
	International	1,534	2,208	
	Total	24,376	26,043	
Riverside	California	43,151	46,456	65.8%
	Out-of-State	1,473	2,492	
	International	4,628	5,417	
	Total	49,252	54,365	
San Diego	California	66,350	84,326	34.3%
	Out-of-State	14,364	23,778	
	International	19,320	23,112	
	Total	100,034	131,226	
Santa Barbara	California	63,269	73,575	29.2%
	Out-of-State	10,988	18,432	
	International	16,690	18,984	
	Total	90,947	110,991	
Santa Cruz	California	43,893	53,051	58.8%
	Out-of-State	3,897	6,878	
	International	7,213	5,937	
	Total	55,003	65,886	

SPOTLIGHT ON THREE PROGRAMS

Georgia Institute of Technology (public, Atlanta, GA)

BS Industrial Design

MID (Masters in Industrial Design)

Georgia Tech's School of Industrial Design has one of the best programs in the country. Tech's research focus offers students a thorough foundation for considering all aspects of the design process as well as inventing new products and technologies. The program seeks "to fortify the designer's role in humanizing connections between people and technology. Through purposeful integration of aesthetic, functional, utilitarian, economic, sustainable, social, and cognitive considerations, our curriculum prepares the new design generation with the tools to develop thoughtful solutions to the challenges of the 21st Century."

Georgia Tech has eleven research labs, the Launchpad Student Showcase, and design competitions like the $20,000 InVenture Prize. Georgia Tech offers opportunities to work with virtual reality. In the Interactive Product Design Lab, students use haptic technologies for car technologies, capacitive touch and motion to track group interactions, sensors to improve post-stroke rehabilitation, and design-centered "smart" products for body scanning, sensor-based technologies, and next-generation wearables.

You will push the boundaries of design in Tech's program with academic study, research projects, and hands-on experiences. The undergraduate program introduces students to a different studio during each of their eight semesters,

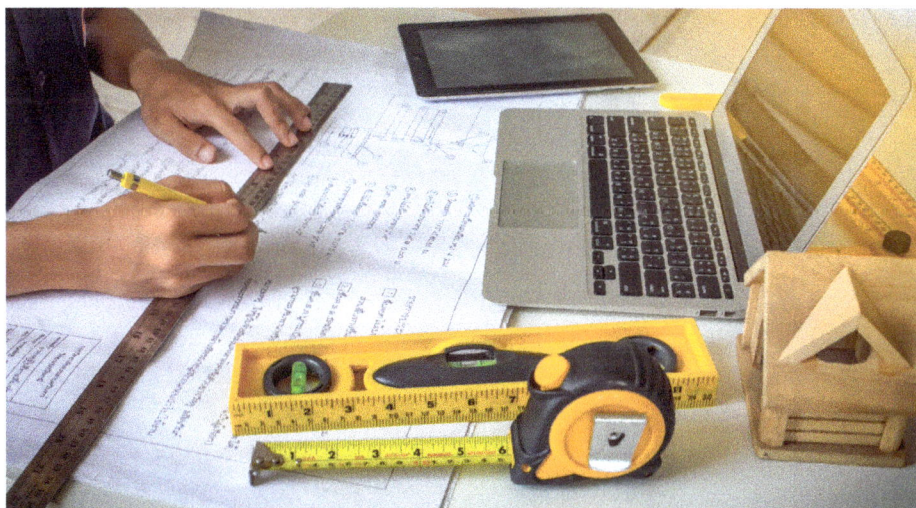

building upon the complexity on a sequential path. They offer specializations in Product Development and Innovation, Health and Well-Being, and Interactive Product Design.

Purdue University (public, West Lafayette, IN)

BFA Industrial Design
MFA Industrial Design

Purdue's Industrial Design major points students towards careers in research and development, project engineering, consulting, toy inventing, or automotive modeler, though there are hundreds of other possibilities. The program is intensive, offering a professional pathway toward manufactured goods design while also preparing students for leadership roles in Industrial Design. While a portfolio is not required upon admission, students must be selected after the portfolio review process at the end of their second year.

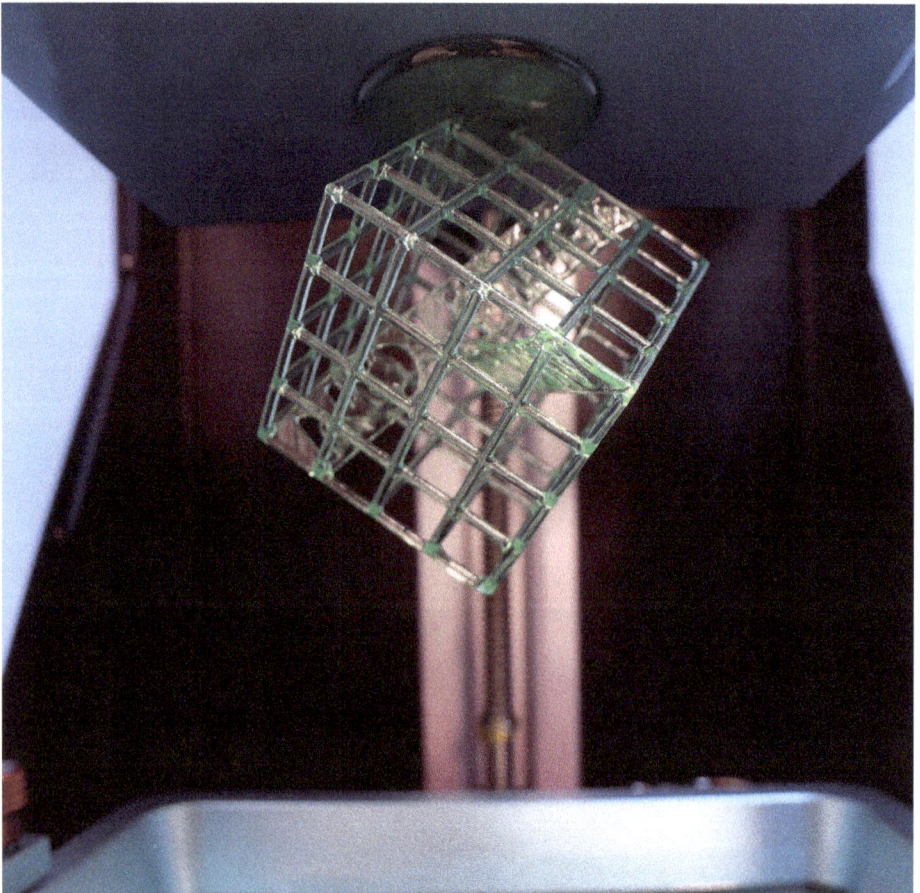

Purdue pushes the boundaries of Industrial Design while teaching students to be a thinker, maker, and innovator. Students have hands-on opportunities to create products for industry. Mixing art and technology, students multitask on projects in 3-D modeling, sketching, and coding. Students do not compete. The atmosphere is collaborative within the college and with companies that partner with the university. Faculty are supportive, helping students find their required internship where they discover and resolve a problem and learn how to manufacture and market the product. Some even extend their learning experience in a job that deepens their skills.

With galleries displaying student projects, there are never-ending examples of state-of-the-art designs. The boat that won the Marine Design grand prize is very cool! The experience design showcase is equally amazing. Designs include digitized leather for children with autism, 'Link' connecting older parents with their children, and a plant growth game. There are also images online to scroll through using the arrow tabs and libraries of images and videos to check out with the VR librarian. Despite the challenging work, students truly seem to enjoy their experience.

Rochester Institute of Technology (private, Rochester, NY)

BFA Industrial Design
MFA Industrial Design

Students develop products throughout their RIT education. In the Fab Lab, students have access to 12 3-D printers as well as laser cutters, CNC routing devices, and power tools. The Center for Additive Manufacturing and Multifunctional Printing allow students to synthesize new functional materials with polymeric, metallic, and ceramic 3-D printing options. RIT offers a Battery Prototyping Center, Center for Human-aware II, Packaging Science Dynamics Lab, Industrial Design Soft Studio Lab, Graphic Design Studio, sewing machines.

One of RIT's focus areas is Personalized Healthcare Technology to create products that improve the lives of others and create devices to empower health. The Golisano Institute for Sustainability offers research opportunities in developing technologies to improve the environment through manufacturing, energy, and transportation.

Students work to create products for athletics, health, and dozens of other items. Student designed projects are currently under production. RIT's Metaproject pairs students with professionals in companies like HermanMiller, Staach, Wilsonart, Corning, Poppin, and Bed Bath & Beyond. Students who are interested in continuing on to study architecture can earn a master's degree in architecture (M.Arch.) along the way.

THE MANY ROADS TO INDUSTRIAL DESIGN SUCCESS

There are numerous ways you can be successful in Industrial Design. The training you get in college can be immensely valuable, particularly while being surrounded by highly skilled practitioners. There is no one road to get to your goal, just as there is not one goal you may want to achieve. Skills in design and manufacturing offer numerous pathways and byways. Some famous designers attended smaller programs where they first gained a broader or more extensive liberal arts education. Exposure to the many different forms of design with students who have diverse interests cannot be understated.

Whichever road you take, enjoy the journey.

CHAPTER 7

COLLEGE DEGREES: TIMING, LOCATION, COSTS, & EARNING POWER

"What a wonderful thought it is that some of the best days of our lives haven't even happened yet."

– Anne Frank

UNDERGRADUATE AND GRADUATE DEGREES

AA – Associate of Arts: 2-year degree

AS – Associate of Science: 2-year degree

BA – Bachelor of Arts: 4-year degree

BArch – Bachelor of Architecture: 5-year professional credential program

BDes – Bachelor of Design: 4-year degree with classes focused on design

BEd – Bachelor of Education: 4-year program focused on teaching & learning

BEng – Bachelor of Engineering: 4-5-year engineering-focused program

BESc – Bachelor of Engineering Science: 4-year science & engineering program

BFA – Bachelor of Fine Arts: 4-year degree with classes focused on art/design

BID – Bachelor of Industrial Design: 4-year Industrial Design-focused degree

BS – Bachelor of Science: 4-year STEM-focused degree

BSCE – Bachelor of Science in Civil Engineering

BS Chem E – Bachelor of Science in Chemical Engineering

BS Comp Sci – Bachelor of Science in Computer Science

BSEE – Bachelor of Science in Electrical Engineering

BSIE – Bachelor of Science in Industrial Engineering

BSME – Bachelor of Science in Mechanical Engineering

EdD – Doctor of Education: 3-5-year program focused on teaching & learning

MA – Master of Arts: 1-2-year specialized degree

MArch – Master of Architecture: 1-3-year professional credential program

MDes – Master of Design: 1-2-year design-focused specialized

MEd – Master of Education: 1-2-year education-focused program

MEng – Master of Engineering: 1-2-year engineering program

MFA – Master of Fine Arts: 1-2-year degree earned after the BA, BS, or BFA

MID – Master of Industrial Design: 1-2-year Industrial Design-focused degree

Minor – Students take 6 to 10 additional classes in an interest area

MS – Master of Science: 1-2-year STEM-focused

MSID – Master of Science in Industrial Design: science-focused Industrial Design

Ph.D. – Doctor of Philosophy: doctorates in any field (typically 3 – 8 years)

AA (ASSOCIATE OF ARTS) & AS (ASSOCIATE OF SCIENCE)

The AA or AS degree is typically a 2-year general studies degree offered online or in-person by a community college. However, some universities offer AA or AS degrees as well. Often, the Associate of Arts degree, while focused on the liberal arts, has no barrier to entry, meaning that students can enter most AA programs with a high school diploma or the equivalent. The AS degree frequently emphasizes science and math and often has additional requirements. Some students take a longer or shorter time to complete the AA based upon their skills upon entering the program, certainty of the direction they are heading, and the transfer requirements for the program they desire. For example, students majoring in business may have additional business, communication, accounting, and economics requirements and need to create an academic plan early in their program to finish in two years.

BA (BACHELOR OF ARTS) & BS (BACHELOR OF SCIENCE)

The BA and BS degrees are 4-year undergraduate degrees that typically offer a liberal arts foundation along with a major or concentration in a specific subject. The BA and BS degrees frequently require students to take lower-division (first and second year) liberal arts courses before taking specialized courses focused around a major or concentration in their third and fourth years.

Although the degrees are primarily offered at liberal arts colleges, art-focused colleges, and universities, a few community colleges offer BA degrees as well. Classes may be taught online or in person. Some students complete their BA in fewer years depending upon AP/ IB credit, dual enrollment, and summer/ intersession classes.

A BFA is considered a professional arts-focused degree with fewer courses in English, science, math, social science, and the humanities. Thus, the BFA, BDes, BID, BArch are specialist qualifications depending upon your art or design focus. The BEng focuses on STEM subjects, while BEd focuses on education. The BA and

BS degrees include significantly more liberal arts classes and thus are more general degrees.

The intention of the BFA, BDes, BID, BArch degrees is for students to pursue a focused curriculum with fewer general subject courses. Finally, a BA or BS are often interchangeable. However, a BFA may be seen as different since there is typically more coursework focused on your specific pursuit with limited broad knowledge and more of a concentration on technical, profession-oriented experiences.

MASTER'S DEGREES & DOCTORAL DEGREES

Both the master's degree and doctorate are specialized, graduate degree programs for students who have completed their bachelor's degree. These degrees can take between one and eight years depending upon coursework, research, practicum, capstone, thesis, qualifying exams, and experiential requirements. Students focus on their field of interest and immerse themselves to gain in-depth practical, coursework, and research training.

I have nine graduate degrees so far and each one is different in what they require and how their classes are designed. However, one consistency is that you graduate with a much deeper knowledge of the specialty. While admission into these programs is generally selective, planning, preparation, and a good portfolio of writing, research, art, publications, or experiences are required. Search for a program that fits your needs. There are numerous options for you to pursue your interests.

THE SEVEN MAJOR DIFFERENCES BETWEEN THE ASSOCIATE, BACHELORS, AND MASTER'S DEGREES

1. Starting Point
2. Academic Discipline
3. Time to Completion
4. Location of the Education
5. Educational Costs
6. Earning Power
7. Professional Opportunities

STARTING POINT

Most students who begin with an Associate of Arts (AA) or Associate of Science (AS) have no college credits. Starting from scratch with their college education, they accumulate their 60+ units beginning from this community college starting point. While most students earn AA or AS degrees at a community college, some earn this degree at a 4-year college or university.

The AA or AS is either a terminal degree, meaning that the student will not continue on with their bachelor's degree or just a steppingstone to their BA, BS, or BFA. The difference between the associate's and bachelor's degrees is just the starting point.

The starting point for students who pursue a bachelor's degree may be farther along the traditional 4-year pathway. Meanwhile, the starting point for the master's degree (MA, MS, or MFA) begins after obtaining a bachelor's degree.

ACADEMIC DISCIPLINE

Every degree encompasses different requirements. Requirements for the AA differ from an AS. Similarly, the requirements for the BA, BS, and BFA also differ. With two additional years of coursework, the BA, BS, and BFA are more thorough. The MA, MS, and MFA build upon the bachelor's degree and even deeper. Students studying Industrial Design will not take the same classes as those pursuing graphic design, though some may overlap. While both are essential to design, the necessary skills for each career area are distinct. Thus, the course requirements are also unique.

Furthermore, with the myriad of combinations, it is rare that any two undergraduate students have the same exact classes in the same exact order. Since the requirements for a chemistry degree are not the same as for biology and Industrial Design differs from graphic design, the various degrees not only include a different number of credits but different types of classes and program specifications.

TIME TO COMPLETION

Associate of Arts (AA) and Associate of Science (AS) degrees typically take two years, while most BA, BS, and BFA degrees are 4-year programs, depending upon full-time or part-time status. Students who transfer in credits or earn credits otherwise can reduce their time to completion.

The time required to earn a bachelor's degree depends upon each student's skills and advanced credit. Still, some students change their direction and chosen major which can add more time. According to the National Center for Educational Statistics, college advisors aid students in finishing "on time" though less than half of all students in the United States who start a bachelor's degree do not finish their degree in four years.[1]

Time in college can be reduced. Some students enter bachelor's degree programs with college credits because they were either dual-enrolled or they took college classes outside of school.

Some students earned qualifying scores on AP/IB tests from taking advanced classes while in high school and were granted credits by the college or university. Policies regarding AP/IB credit vary. Look on each school website. Other ways students can enter at a different starting point are with credit-by-exam, CLEP tests, experiential credits, and those granted in the military.

Colleges and universities are keenly aware of the challenges students face today with work, illness, and family responsibilities. Thus, many schools of higher education offer flexible enrollment with opportunities for part-time, evening, weekend, and online classes.

---

1   IEC NCES, "Digest of Education Statistics, Table 326.10," IES NCES, n.d., https://nces.ed.gov/programs/digest/d20/tables/dt20_326.10.asp?referer=raceindica.asp

LOCATION OF THE EDUCATION

The AA and AS are earned at colleges that grant 2-year degrees. The location may be at a local community college or a university. BA, BS, and BFA programs are offered at a 4-year college or university. However, with online classes, students have the flexibility to take classes from colleges farther away as well. Thus, the location in which a typical student studies is not as set as it once was. Nevertheless, the in-person internships are often situated in corporate hubs and thus require grounding to a specific location.

EDUCATIONAL COSTS

Since the AA or AS requires a shorter amount of time and is typically completed at a lower-cost community college, the cost for an associate's degree is typically less than a bachelor's degree. Master's degree programs cost more per credit but take less time than a bachelor's degree.

On the other hand, many students can obtain financial aid in the form of grants, loans, and both merit and need-based scholarships. This aid can pay for school and reduce debt after college.

We must be willing to let go of the life we planned
to have the life that is waiting for us.

- Joseph Campbell

EARNING POWER

Students with more education can earn more. According to the 2019 National Center for Educational Statistics (NCES) data for the median person,[2]

- Master's Degree or Higher - $70,000
- Bachelor's Degree - $55,700
- Associate's Degree - $43,300
- High School - $35,000

There is a wide range in annual salaries from those who have consistent contracts and are paid six-digit or seven-digit salaries to those who earn less than $20,000. Thus, the average salary may seem low since the variation is huge.

PROFESSIONAL OPPORTUNITIES

Earning a BA, BS, BDes, BID, or BFA opens more doors than an AA or AS. Similarly, an MA, MS, MDes, MID, or MFA opens more doors than a BA, BS, or BFA. Baccalaureate and master's degrees require more training. You can obtain this training through workshops or studio classes, but with a scholarship to pay for college, you might find that the training and opportunities are worth your time. Besides, you will gain additional skills that could prove valuable in your future.

---

2   IES NCES, "Annual Earnings by Educational Attainment," IEC NCES, May 2021, https://nces.ed.gov/programs/coe/indicator/cba

The beautiful thing about learning is that no one can take it from you.

- **B.B. King**

Professional opportunities depend upon your specific interest and country, like Canada, China, Italy, Japan, and South Korea. Many industrial design companies cross over into product design, packaging design, strategy, engineering, AR, VR, and promotional branding. However, some focus on industrial/product design, prototyping, and small batch manufacturing. Scroll through the firms that belong to the Industrial Designers Society of America and Dexigner to get a sense of more than 100 professional options available to you.

Company size may also be a factor in your decision-making. While large firms may have more diversity of function and upward mobility, you might also be tasked with a specialized or limited role. On the other hand, a smaller firm may give you the chance to multitask on a wide range of projects and have a greater stake in the big picture of the operation. Whatever you decide, by taking internships in firms large and small, you will discover your preferences and, at a minimum, know the questions to ask during interviews.

IoT design combines hardware and software in an integrated system that allows computers to monitor, collect data, relay information, and revise processes. This specialization transforms product ideas into comprehensive strategies into networks to embed, sense, and track, providing more ubiquitous flow into consumer and cloud-based interactions. In addition, new home and office devices are more sustainable with specs that allow individuals or companies to 3D print parts for quicker repair.

Law school might be another direction you could take your education. One of the biggest challenges facing designers is the control of their intellectual property. While filing for a patent is not terribly difficult, maintaining control of that property is much more challenging. In our copycat world, globalization delivers products worldwide to places that do not conform to international law. Products are taken apart, reconfigured or modified, and put back onto the market. Some firms focus on protecting intellectual property by seeking out and prosecuting violators.

Jump at chances to gain real-world experiences. You may be in the workforce for fifty years. That is a really long time if you do not feel fulfilled. Sure, internships may mean sacrificing a summer holiday for a month somewhere, but it could make a significant difference in your life.

CHAPTER 8

COLLEGE ADMISSIONS: APPLICATIONS, ESSAYS, RECOMMENDATIONS, CHECKLISTS, AND ADVICE

"We all have ability. The difference is how we use it."

– Stevie Wonder

PRESIDENT'S VOLUNTEER SERVICE AWARD

There is no money for this award, but it is nonetheless important to share. Individuals submit their community service hours and win these awards.

Hours Required to Earn Awards in Each Age Group

Age Group	Bronze	Silver	Gold	Lifetime Achievement Award
Kids (5–10 years old)	26–49 hours	50–74 hours	75+ hours	4,000+ hours
Teens (11–15)	50–74 hours	75–99 hours	100+ hours	4,000+ hours
Young Adults (16–25)	100–174 hours	175–249 hours	250+ hours	4,000+ hours
Adults (26+)	100–249 hours	250–499 hours	500+ hours	4,000+ hours

COLLEGE ADMISSIONS:

Success in the Face of Uncertainty

There are no guarantees in college admissions. However, planning is essential for success. The most beneficial advice is to pursue your passions with gusto, train to be the best you can be, take advantage of internships and experiences, and meet lots of people along the way.

Remember, "life is a journey, not a destination." Often the journey is more exciting, leading to lessons, friendships, and unforgettable moments. However, the fact is, in the end, if college is your goal, then you need to know a few action items to remember for success.

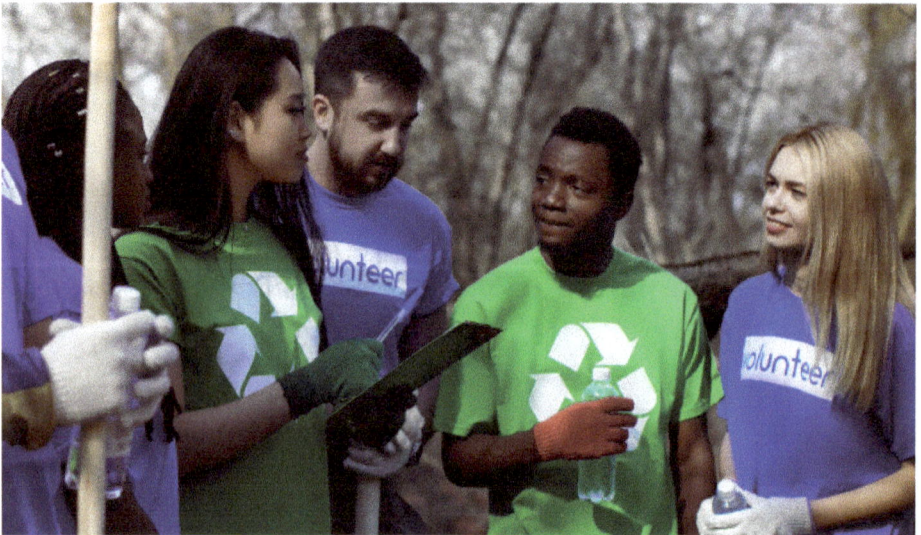

Should you worry about grades? Of course. You should also take classes that will challenge you. Colleges pick the best candidates from those who apply. Students must be academically prepared, socially conscious, and talented in a few different areas in which they are passionate (design, graphic arts, musical instruments, theatre, debate, public speaking, leadership, athletics, community service, computer coding, robotics, construction, etc.).

The college selection process is not that much different than companies picking employees. While colleges are more or less competitive, companies may have only one job, and a hundred resumes. Discover the unique drive and internal motivations within you that make you the very best you can be. Be exceptional at what you choose to do academically, personally, and professionally.

Most of all, You Do You

TALENT FOCUSED

Not all schools require high grades and test scores. Many are simply interested in selecting students who are the most talented, most driven, and the most willing to be team players on the college campus. Thus, you should take a solid set of courses and fulfill the standard requirements.

Hundreds of thousands of students attend college with GPAs between 2.5 and 3.5. Furthermore, most college students today, more than ten million never take standardized tests. If you are applying to highly competitive schools, you should take the test. However, there are hundreds of colleges that do not require test scores in 2022 and probably never will in the future.

In a comprehensive April 22, 2022, report,[1] Melanie Hanson of the Education Data Initiative did a fabulous job presenting copious educational data. I pulled some that you may find informative.

In 2020, total college enrollment was approximately 19 million, dropping by two million from its high in 2010 with 3.1 million in graduate school. Approximately one-third (66.2%) of high school students go on for post-secondary study. California has the most college students with 2.72 million; 89.5% attend public institutions; 11.6% leave the state to attend college; 35.8% of full time college students are female.

---

1   Melanie Hanson. "College Enrollment & Student Demographic Statistics" EducationData.org, April 22, 2022, https://educationdata.org/college-enrollment-statistics

In approximate numbers, here is some college student data.

DEMOGRAPHIC CHARACTERISTICS

Caucasian – 54.3%

LatinX - 19.3%

Black or African American - 12.6%

Asian or Asian American – 6.8%

American Indian/Alaska Native – 0.66%%

Pacific Islander – 0.26%

Foreign-born – 12%

Women - 55.5%

15 years old or younger – 0.7%

Under 24 years old – 92%

45 years old or older – 1.5%

DEGREES AND MAJORS

4.43 million students graduated in 2021

* 24.6% received associate's degrees

* 49.9% received bachelor's degrees

* 20.8% earned master's degrees

* 4.7% earned doctorates/professional degrees

Majors – 58% of all bachelor's degrees are in five areas of study

* 19.1% in business

* 11.9% in health-related professions

* 8% social sciences and history

* 5.9% in psychology

* 5.9% in biological and biomedical sciences

COMPETITIVE COLLEGE ADMISSIONS

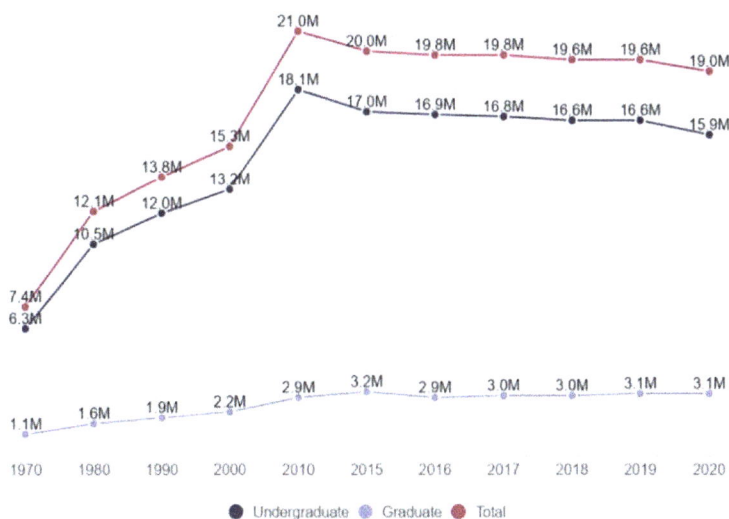

21.0M
20.0M   19.8M   19.8M   19.6M   19.6M
18.1M   19.0M
17.0M   16.9M   16.8M   16.6M   16.6M
15.3M   15.9M
13.8M
13.2M
12.1M   12.0M
10.5M
7.4M
6.3M

1.1M   1.6M   1.9M   2.2M   2.9M   3.2M   2.9M   3.0M   3.0M   3.1M   3.1M

1970   1980   1990   2000   2010   2015   2016   2017   2018   2019   2020

● Undergraduate ● Graduate ● Total

A few highly selective colleges seek extraordinary talent over academics, but most zero in on a student's challenging courses and high grades. To gain admission into the most highly selective academic colleges, you must take the most challenging course load you can manage and succeed. Highly selective colleges want disciplined scholars AND remarkably talented students.

Determine what you can handle, knowing that some colleges with extremely competitive admission will only take students who have completed more than ten AP, IB, or honors classes over the four years.

Why would the most competitive colleges require classes like AP Calculus or Physics for an art program? However daunting these classes may seem, remember, the top colleges have lots of applicants, and they need to draw the line somewhere. UCLA had 149,779 applicants for fall 2022; UC Berkeley had 128,192 applicants. The numbers are truly staggering since neither first-year class will have no have more than 7,000 students starting in the fall.

College admissions can feel like a rollercoaster of energy and emotion. Creating a portfolio of talent, training, and experience is just the beginning. Meanwhile, some colleges want to see standardized test scores aided by practice. Applications and essays may seem easy at first, but managing the various requirements and deadlines can be difficult. Therefore, this moment is a good time to get a calendar and organize your tasks.

REQUEST INFORMATION

Almost every college has a location, a link, or a contact us page where you can request information from the school. If you are considering a school, request information from them. In this way, they may send you updates, scholarship opportunities, a valuable application fee waiver, special invites, and other information that could be valuable in the process. Of course, you may not need one more e-mail, and you may be receiving e-mails from the school anyway. Still, I recommend that you fill out their form. Then, since you are likely to be inundated with e-mails, make a file folder in your e-mail for all colleges you are considering. Then, when you get an e-mail from one of those schools, file it away.

STANDARDIZED TESTING

A few schools still require standardized testing. Check first. Many colleges are test-optional. This means that you are not required to take the SAT or ACT. However, if you have a good score, it may make all the difference in gaining admission. College admissions offices are studying this topic and considering their future policies. Much of their concern began with test cancelations worldwide due to the pandemic.

Schools did not want to let students into their site to take the test who may be infected, nor were they able to ensure safety. In addition, social distancing requirements limited the number of students who could take a test at any given

site. Yet, for decades, college admissions decisions centered around grades and test scores. This change in the landscape of decision-making has rattled admissions departments.

Meanwhile, some colleges proclaim that test-optional truly means that the test is not required. Yet, evidence proves otherwise. Thus, many students are still taking the test and working around the hurdles amid the confusion. Competition continues to drive students to present evidence to show that they are worthy candidates. In the end, colleges need to make a final decision between very good candidates. If one student has a high score, that student may have a higher likelihood of admission depending upon the admissions committee's decision-making process.

Data show that students who submitted scores within the college's range or higher were accepted at a higher rate than those without a score. Some schools are test blind in that they say that they do not consider your scores. A few of these colleges still provide a place to input your scores. Thus, they are not truly blind. Nevertheless, the decision regarding whether you take the test or submit the score is yours. If the school does not require an admissions test, you can choose to take the test and submit it as you like. If your academics are solid and you are willing to prepare for the test, you should take the test.

APPLYING EARLY
Early Action (EA), Restricted Early Action (REA), and Early Decision (ED)

With low acceptance rates, the chance to get more scholarship money, and the chaos surrounding the cancellations and changes in AP, IB, SAT, and ACT testing, students clamor to apply early to schools. In addition, applications to the top schools increased during the pandemic, resulting in colleges needing to make difficult admissions decisions in their quest to build a diverse, talented, and engaged class of students. Furthermore, students applying early have access to many more scholarship options. This confluence sent students in droves to apply early. This trend is likely to continue.

In Early Action (EA), Restricted Early Action (REA), and Early Decision (ED), students apply in late summer or early fall to college and generally find out around winter break, though some decisions come out earlier and a few arrive later. This advantage not only gives students a chance for more scholarship money in some cases but the benefit of finding out early reduces the tension of the long waiting period to find out about Regular Decision schools.

Early Action (EA) and Restricted Early Action (REA) are different. In restricted early action, a limitation is placed on either how many or what colleges you can apply to simultaneously. Many REA schools do not allow students to apply to other early action schools, though some will allow students to apply early to public colleges. Check the colleges to be sure. In addition, some schools like Georgetown will allow students to apply EA elsewhere but not apply to a binding Early Decision (ED) program where the student commits to attending if they are accepted. However, most EA schools do not have these restrictions, and some students apply to a handful of EA schools during the admissions process.

Early Decision (ED) is a binding agreement between the student and college with signatures from the student's parents and the high school assuring that the student is committed and will attend. Each of these parties acknowledges and agrees that, if granted admission, they will fulfill their agreement. There are caveats to this, though you should go into the agreement fully committing to your ED school.

There are incentives to applying ED. Frequently, acceptance rates are higher. Also, at some schools, a large percentage of their class is filled with students who profess their unequivocal love for their dream school. Students who know they have a top choice school, have the necessary admissions prerequisites fulfilled, and are committed to accepting the binding agreement to attend, should apply ED.

COMMON APPLICATION, COALITION APPLICATION, OR COLLEGE-SPECIFIC APPLICATION

Every college's process is unique. However, there are a few commonalities. In 2022, approximately 900 colleges used the Common App; about 150 colleges used the Coalition Application. A few used both. The University of California system has its own application as do the California State Universities and the Texas schools.

The Common App and Coalition App may be started early. In your junior year, consider getting a head start on reviewing what is required. The college-specific questions may change each year. However, the basic application is generally the same and can be created ahead of time. At the end of July, make a copy of everything you have completed just in case.

Some schools admit on a rolling basis. 'Rolling' means that periodically, after all of the materials are received, the admissions committee determines who they will accept, and they send the notification right away. Some students are accepted as early as August. The thrill of acceptance cannot be overstated.

ADMISSIONS TERMS TO KNOW

Admissions Tests – These are tests like SAT, ACT, GMAT, GRE, MCAT, etc. that universities use to standardize student's aptitude in foundational academic skill areas.

Admit Rate – The percent of applicants who are admitted.

Articulation Agreement – This is the agreement between 2-year and 4-year colleges that determines whether credits transfer from one institution to another.

Candidate Reply Date – For freshman admissions, students must reply back to colleges by May 1 with their choice of college or university they will attend from those in which they were accepted.

Class Rank – Most high schools no longer rank students. However, a few still do. This ranking puts students in order of weighted GPA. Some schools rank in percentiles or deciles.

Coalition Application – This standardized application app can be sent to multiple schools within the network of approximately 150 colleges. Most colleges also require supplemental applications with additional essays and requirements.

College Credit – Most colleges require 120 – 130 semester credits to graduate with a bachelor's degree. Students earn credits upon successful completion of classes. Colleges may award college credit for qualifying AP/IB scores, CLEP exams, and military training courses.

Common Application – This is a standardized application app that can be sent to multiple schools within the network of approximately 900 colleges. Most colleges also require supplemental applications with additional essays and requirements.

Deferred Admission – After the EA/ED admissions cycle, students are accepted, denied, or deferred to regular decision. Typically, the chances of being accepted during the regular admissions cycle after being deferred is 5–10%.

Deferred Enrollment – Colleges allow a student to postpone their attendance for up to one year. Note: Not all colleges allow students to defer.

Domestic Student – Students who are U.S. residents no matter where they live. Some schools reserve this term for U.S. citizens who are out-of-state students.

Early Action (EA) – An early application submission in which a student also finds out their decision before regular decisions. Early action is not binding, meaning that students do not need to enroll if accepted. Most EA application due dates are between October 15th and November 15th. Almost all EA decisions come back between December 1st and February 1st with most responses between December 10th – 20th.

Early Decision (ED) – A few colleges have ED whereby a student commits to one school should they be accepted. Students agree to attend when they apply, and they can only apply to one ED school. If admitted, students pay the deposit and withdraw their applications from other schools. ED applications are typically due November 1 and decisions typically come back in mid-December.

Financial Aid – This is money given to help pay for school and can be composed of scholarships, grants, loans, and work-study. Financial aid may be granted from the government, college, or private organizations.

First-Generation – Students are 'first-gen' if neither of their parents has a four-year college degree. Some states differ and say that the parents of first-gen students never attended college.

High School GPA – This number is recalculated differently by each college depending upon whether they include 9th – 11th, summers, middle school, AP/IB/Honors credit, and courses like health, computer applications, leadership, sports, etc. Some colleges like the University of California cap their weighted GPA for admissions purposes with only 8 semesters of 'honors' points. No more than 4 of these can be from 10th grade.

In-State – These students are students who have residency in the state (driver's license, taxes, etc.) no matter where they physically live.

International – These applicants are not residents of the United States in the eyes of admissions. For some students, this designation varies from state to state.

Legacy – A child with a close relative who graduated from a given college. Some colleges give preference to legacy applicants.

Lower Division – These are courses typically taken in your first two years of college. Most community college classes are lower division. At a university, lower division courses for a BA or BS degree are primarily liberal arts classes.

Need-Aware Admissions – The policy where admissions teams consider financial circumstances in the admissions process.

Need-Blind Admissions – The policy where admissions teams do not consider financial circumstances in the admissions process.

Open Admissions – A college opens enrollment to all students until the seats are filled without consideration of past academic performance.

Placement Tests – Most colleges require certain levels of mastery before entering a class. Upon enrolling in a college, students take placement tests to determine the level in which they are placed. Since information recall may not be strong from a class taken years before, you should review the material before you take the test or you may need to take one or two additional remedial classes which may prolong graduation.

Portal – This is the online center where you log in to determine what the college is missing (transcripts, test scores, portfolio, etc.), scholarships, and your admissions status.

Registrar's Office – This is the office of college officials who are responsible for your student records - recording grades, certifying completion, and sending transcripts.

Residency – This is the determination of state residency, non-resident U.S., or international.

Rolling Admission – This is the college policy to accept students as the applications come into the school rather than waiting for a specific date. Many colleges with rolling admissions will determine your admission to the school within a month of receipt of your materials.

Summer Melt – The phenomenon whereby students submit an intent to enroll at a college after being admitted, pay the deposit, and decide not to attend during the summer. While this situation may have increased during the pandemic, the phenomenon has recurred for decades. The primary reasons for summer melt include the inability to pay, illness, family matter, change of heart, acceptance of a job, or getting off the waitlist at another college.

Transfer Student – A student who has taken college classes after completing high school and applies to a 4-year university. Typically, college classes taken during high school still allow students to apply for freshman admissions.

Upper Division – These are courses typically taken in your second two years of college. At a university, upper division courses for a BA or BS degree are primarily major-specific classes.

Waitlist – Admissions offices accept, deny, or waitlist students. Those students on a waitlist must wait until a spot opens. If there is a vacancy, the student may be taken off of the waitlist on a priority basis, ranking system, or admissions review.

Yield – This is the percent of admitted students who pay the deposit with the intent to enroll (enrolled/admitted x 100).

ESSAYS

The Common Application and Coalition essays are often posted months ahead of time. Since this main essay is required or recommended for nearly all Common Application and Coalition Application schools, this is an excellent place to start thinking about what you might want to say to colleges.

In addition to the main essay on the Common Application and Coalition Application, about three-fours of the colleges have their own specific questions or essays. In August, most admissions applications are open and ready for you to dive into the college-specific questions, though many of the essay topics are available earlier, and some schools hold out until later for their big essay reveal.

These can be prepared ahead of time too. One popular question is, "What activity is most important to you and why?" Another is "Why did you choose your major?" A third common question is, "Why do you want to attend our school?" Others you should prepare or at least consider the topics of diversity, adversity, and challenges since these topics have become increasingly important in the admissions process. Everyone has a challenge they needed to overcome. What did you learn from that experience?

Complete the application fully. Think carefully about optional sections. Typically, universities offer you the chance to provide the school with just the right cherry on top of the sundae, allowing you to share something unique about you. If you have absolutely nothing to say, leave it blank. There is an additional information section on the main Common App, Coalition Application, and University of California application. This location is not a place to write another essay, but you can include information that cannot be adequately explained in the rest of the application.

There are also schools that include scholarship essays within the supplement part of the application. Start early.

LETTERS OF RECOMMENDATION

Most colleges, though not all, request letters of recommendation from a counselor and one or more teachers. The university may want academic teachers and art teachers for drawing and painting programs. Plan for this. Occasionally, there is a section for optional recommendations too. In this location, you might get a recommendation from a summer program leader or someone with whom you did an internship. If you were in a sport, there is a location for a coach on about a quarter of the applications. Finally, if there is a supplemental application, for example, on SlideRoom, these often require separate recommendations reviewed by the art program.

COLLEGE APPLICATION CHECKLIST

☐ Calendar - Keep a calendar of due dates for summer program applications, contests, AP tests, SAT/ACT, applications, scholarships, and financial aid.

☐ Career Interest Survey - Take a career interest/aptitude test. Learn more about the majors and career options that best fit your interests and abilities

☐ Consider College Majors – What classes are offered in the curriculum? Many students who dislike math are surprised to learn that most business degrees require both calculus and statistics while incorporating math in nearly every class. It pays to research the subjects now.

☐ Investigate Colleges – Consider possible schools based on the programs they offer, research opportunities, internships, clubs, activities, sports, and personal interests - visit if possible.

☐ National College Fair – In the spring, colleges send representatives to a couple of dozen cities where you can meet with their admissions staff. These are good to walk around and learn more about the colleges and ask questions.

☐ Request Information – Fill out the request for information for each college you are considering so that they keep you informed of opportunities you may not have considered. They may send you a fee waiver or streamlined application.

☐ Summer Programs – Summer camps, skill-building, tours, research, internships, and college programs often have deadlines. Apply and consider your options.

☐ Narrow Choices – Narrow down your choices in the summer before your senior year so that you have an equal number of target, reach, and safeties.

☐ Communicate With Your Counselor – Your counselor is your guide who not only helps you with your course selection but also advocates for you in the admissions process through their recommendation and sometimes with admissions. Get to know them.

- ☐ **SAT/ACT** – Decide if there is a benefit of taking these tests for the colleges you are considering.

- ☐ **Extended Time** – Determine if you qualify for extended time on tests.

- ☐ **Fee Waivers** – Ask your counselor if you qualify for fee waivers for the SAT/ACT, CSS Profile, or application fees.

- ☐ **Resume** – Create a resume whether or not the college requests one – some do. First, you may need one for a job. However, a resume allows you to gather your activities and accomplishments in one place for you to see what you want to present to a school.

- ☐ **Essays and Short Answer Questions** – Determine aspects of your life that stand out. Give colleges the best impression of your interests, inspirations, commitment, and life journey.

- ☐ **Counselor Recommendation Form** – Determine if your school requires a special form to obtain a counselor recommendation.

- ☐ **Recommendations** – Ask your teachers in the spring of your junior year or when school starts in your senior year.

- ☐ **Early Action/Early Decision** – These applications are due first, typically between October 15th and November 15th.

- ☐ **Regional Representative** – Some colleges have a regional representative. If you have any specifications, contact them to have them answer questions you cannot find the answers to on the website.

- ☐ **Transcripts** – Order transcripts to be sent to colleges from your high school (s) and any colleges you have attended. Note: Some colleges like the University of California do not want transcripts sent until you are admitted.

- ☐ **Deadlines** – Keep your eye on the deadlines.

- ☐ **Portals** – You must log into your portal after you submit your application and then every couple of weeks afterward to see if the college is missing something from your file. Some colleges will close your application if you do not log in or will move your early application to regular decision.

- ☐ **Scholarships** – Scholarships vary in due dates. Some begin the process of considering students in the spring of your junior year. The Coca-Cola Scholarship is due October 31st. However, due dates continue throughout most of your senior year. Scan www.fastweb.com and www.bigfuture.collegeboard.org/scholarship-search.

- ☐ **Regular Decision** – Regular decision applications for public colleges vary, but many are right after Thanksgiving. Regular decision application deadlines for most private schools are the first two weeks of January.

- ☐ **FAFSA** – Apply for federal financial aid (grants, work study, and loans).

- ☐ **CSS Profile** – About 300 colleges require this form to obtain financial aid.

- ☐ **Student Aid Report (SAR)** – Approximately 4 weeks after completing your FAFSA you should receive your SAR. Follow the instructions to complete updates or add schools.

- ☐ **Update Colleges** – Make sure you update colleges with your continued interest.

- ☐ **Keep Copies** – Keep copies of your application materials in a folder.

- ☐ **Visit Colleges** – If possible, visit colleges to which you were accepted. Since you are going to live there for four years, you should get a feel for the campus and not just judge a school by its rankings.

- ☐ **Communicate With Students** – Find students who currently attend the university who are willing to answer a few questions. How hard is it to change your major? Are students friendly? What do students do on the weekends? As your counselor, teachers, or the admissions office if they can refer you to a student who currently attends or just graduated.

- ☐ **Waitlisted Schools** – Most schools will allow you to write a letter updating them on your accomplishments during your senior year and your continued interest. Read the instructions since every school has a different format and set of requirements. Demonstrate your commitment.

- ☐ **Candidate Reply Date** – By May 1st you must choose one school and place a deposit.

- ☐ **Senior Year Grades** – Colleges rescind admissions offers for students who do poorly in their senior year. Do not slack off. You will regret it.

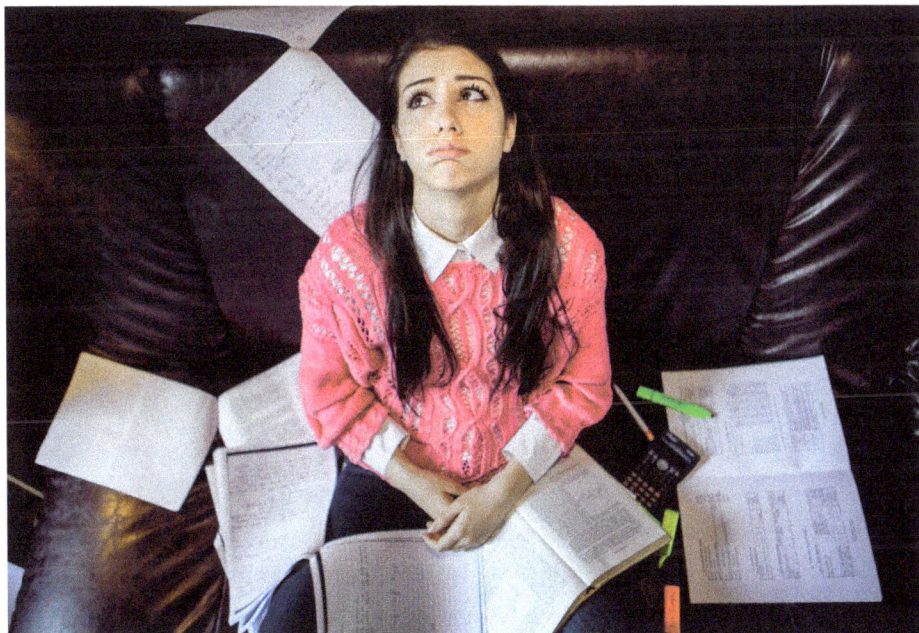

DECISIONS, DECISIONS: WAITING FOR A RESPONSE

The period between submitting your application and getting your admissions results may not require a tremendous amount of work, but it does require patience and diligence. First, most schools will send you a link to a portal where you will check your results, though the most important reason for checking every couple of weeks is to ensure that the college is not missing something or has not offered you the chance to apply for an extra scholarship.

Check your portal regularly. Otherwise, read the college's correspondence sent through your e-mail. Waiting is difficult. These few months are a tough period because students want to know. However, the college typically lists the date they will send out the results on the portal. Other popular sites post their decision notification dates too. You will find out soon.

THICK OR THIN ENVELOPE

Students clamor for the mail each spring waiting to hear via e-mail, the college portal, or the mail - welcome packet or denial letter. You know spring has come as regular decision admissions results steadily roll, one at a time. In March, every day seems to last 26 hours, two extra for the period that lingers until that day's announcement. With each school announcing on a different day, the slow drip torture waiting to find out is exacerbated by the uncanny way each college picks a different day in March to announce their decision.

At some point you will know. That statement seems like little solace in the middle of the fray. You have until May 1 to make a decision, though with limited housing available and a first-come, first-served basis of selection, the pressure is on to choose. Even so, visiting the college is vital, despite the fact that AP tests and finals are just around the corner and there seems like there is no time. However, this decision is where you will live, eat, study, make friends, take classes, and get involved for four years. If you do not consider your options, you are basing your decision on a few college-selected pictures and the tweets or feeds of other people.

There are many variables to consider in the end. This is why forward thinking at the beginning of the application process is valuable and even necessary to seek scholarships, merit money, or opportunities for financial aid. This proactive planning is especially needed with the spike in college applications at selective schools and the ever-changing landscape of test-optional admissions. MIT, for example, resumed its test requirement.

Plan ahead. The college application process is not a good time to procrastinate. The fall of your senior year is tough, often with a demanding course load. It is even tougher for athletes who compete in a fall sport. However, throughout your life you will need to work on time management, organization, and goal setting. This is a good time to start so you do not miss thousands of dollars in financial aid. Time management challenged students who adjusted their lifestyles due the self-paced and online classes and assignments during the pandemic.

CELEBRATING ACCEPTANCES AND DEALING WITH REJECTION

Acceptance is not guaranteed. The probabilities are low at the most highly selective schools. However, you just need to work hard in school to have what it takes and give this commitment to academics all you have. When you find out the results, you will celebrate your acceptances.

Congratulations! The colleges in which you gain admission go on your list of wins. Check your financial aid and scholarship packages too. Money is often an important factor in making your decision. Consider visiting the school. Many students apply to college merely by someone's recommendation, *U.S. News and World Report* ranking, looking at campus photos on Google, or researching profiles posted on a website or in a book.

There is nothing that replaces the actual campus visit. After all, you will be spending a few years there. While you may not be accepted everywhere you apply, you may decide when you visit that the college is high on your list or that you do not want to apply after all. Understandably, the pandemic's uncertainty added more question marks to an already complicated set of admissions processes.

The buzzword for 2020-2030 is resilience. It is never easy to be rejected. However, rejection happens, and you will survive this. Note that many colleges still accept applications in April, May, and June long after most school's applications are closed. Look up those colleges if you did not get accepted or if you want to see what other schools might be good options for you. In April and May, Google "College Openings Update". You will be surprised to see the colleges that show up on the list that still have open spots.

WAITLISTS: THE ART OF WAITING

Immediately confirm if you are given a waitlist spot and still want to attend. There is often a deadline. You do not want to miss this. If you are no longer interested or have selected another school, go into the portal and turn down the offer. Someone else is bound to be thrilled by your anonymous gift.

If you are still interested, find the location on the portal or site designated by the college to update them on what you have done – accomplishments, awards, extra class, honors, art, shows, or films. You only want to add what they have not yet seen, but if you have taken the initiative to do something more than what you originally stated on the application, by all means, tell them.

You could just wait for their decision, but you are better off being proactive and showing that you really want to be at their school. Students do get off the waitlists at most schools. How much do you want to attend? Meanwhile, you will have to deposit somewhere else before the May 1st deadline. Stay hopeful. This next year will be a significant step along your journey. Relax!

ACCEPTANCE IS JUST THE BEGINNING

Once you are accepted to college, you begin your journey toward your future. They call graduation "commencement" because you start your trek on your own path. The decisions you make now are primarily yours with significantly less input from your parents. For better or worse, your parents taught you lessons that you will keep or discard. Now, your behaviors, attitudes, internships, study abroad, and career choices will determine what you become.

Warning ahead of time…the path is rarely straight and there are pitfalls along the way. Much like Monopoly, you will roll the dice and move ahead a few squares, but you will go back a few spaces as well. You might buy a house. You might collect some cash; you might lose some too. Life is full of lessons. Successful adults can sometimes look back and forget about the wrong turns because they sting at the time and then they are dismissed over the years as lessons.

I have literally been in college for nearly fifty years and have degrees that span a multitude of disciplines. I have also taught chemistry, mathematics, engineering, counseling, public relations, and politics. Here are twenty-one tips as you go forward.

1. Attend class even when other students don't. Surprisingly, many lecture halls are half empty when there isn't a test. Go anyway. Most college professors know if you attend.

2. Buy your books and start reading before the semester starts. When classes begin, you live in a blizzard of activities, opportunities, and assignments. Again, surprisingly, most students do not complete their assigned readings. Some get by without reading but getting As that way is tough.

3. Work ahead. Finish your paper or project first, then go out and celebrate your friend's birthday, sports team win, or friend-group's successes. Not only can you be more relaxed, but you might even improve on your work later when you come up with a new idea.

4. Most colleges offer free tutoring. The tutors will read over your paper or assignment and almost always give you valuable assistance that you would never have considered. Return to #3, to do this you must complete your assignment ahead of time.

5. Have a backup plan or two. Murphy's Law say: (1) Anything that can go wrong will, (2) Nothing is as easy as it looks, (3) Everything takes longer than you think it will.

6. Save your documents – often. The worst thing is when you lose a file, your computer turns off or malware attacks your files. Google Drive is fine for some things, but there are pitfalls.

7. Develop a solid notetaking system that works for you. You will need it for the rest of your life. Small things slip through the cracks. Checklists are extremely helpful.

8. There is never enough time. Bring enough clothes so you do not need to wash them as often. When you do wash them, take them out when they are done or else someone else will and you may never find them again.

9. Register for classes the minute the classes open up for you. Trust me on this one. Otherwise, you get a bad professor at a horrible time that conflicts with your commitments. You might not even get into prerequisites which extend your time in college.

10. Petition to get into a class. Begging is fine. The professor can say no, but at least you tried.

11. If you have any academic problem with illness, family, or an emergency, let your professors know immediately. Most will not care if you wait for a month thinking that you can handle it on your own.

12. Make a calendar and keep track of what you need to accomplish.

13. Teamwork is a mantra in college. You will work on teams. A few members are likely to be unmotivated slackers or talented, but extreme procrastinators. Determine this ahead of time and set intermediate goals. Remember, your grade is on the line. It's not fair but go back to #5. In the end, finish the project anyway. The unmotivated slacker will get an A, which may thoroughly make you frustrated, but you will too.

14. Book prices vary widely. The bookstore at the university is often not the cheapest. I have friends who swear by certain places where they always buy textbooks, get coupons, and then buy more books. However, the advantage of buying books in digital format is that you can often Control F information you need and sometimes take digital notes, which is impossible with a physical copy. I prefer physical books, but you choose. Also, renting books is okay unless you forget to send the book back.

15. Get involved as soon as you can. Meet students who have similar interests. Join clubs, learn about the school's traditions, try activities you always wanted to learn, ask professors about volunteering on research projects, and get involved with intramural sports.

16. Don't bring a car. A car sounds wonderful, offering you freedom until your vehicle is broken into, the gas runs out, the car breaks down before a test, or you get a half dozen parking tickets. You never realized how much trouble a car could be on campus where there is limited and expensive parking.

17. Communicate with your professors. Most of them have office hours. Well, they probably all have office hours, but sometimes they are absent. Either drop by or make an appointment. Especially if you have a question or a problem, speak to them. A professor rarely helps a student after they turn in grades but may have excellent advice during the term if they are struggling. Surprisingly, also sometimes, the answer key is wrong. Occasionally, they are intimidating, standoffish, or mean-spirited. Fortunately, there are only a few bad ones, and even these professors teach you important lessons.

18. Don't get so excited about credit cards. Credit card companies will continually hound you to sign up with tempting offers. College students are prime targets because they do not yet really understand how challenging it is to pay them off monthly when there are so many things to purchase. You will probably have to learn the hard way, but they are not the savior they purport to be. Furthermore, you will likely spend more than you imagined, and the interest payments will dig you into a deep hole.

19. Drinking and drugs are around you 24/7. It does not matter what school you attend. Rarely is a campus void of alcohol or drugs. However, some colleges have more – much more. Some students will even sell illegal drugs in the dorm. You need to use your own judgment. Be careful. Students consume more than they realize, make judgment errors, get seriously injured, die of overdoses, and spread STDs. This piece was not written to scare you but to make you aware of the life-changing realities.

20. During Christmas break starting your first year, apply for internships, training opportunities, co-ops, or jobs for the summer. Create a resume. Getting experience cannot be understated if you want to jump on the job market and get real-world experience. Career fairs are extremely helpful so you can see what kind of job you might want. Every college has a career center. Get to know the people there.

21. Go boldly into this world and try new things. Thomas Edison once said, "I have not failed. I've just found 10,000 ways that won't work."

CHAPTER 9

FINANCIAL AID AND SCHOLARSHIPS

"If you are not willing to risk the usual, you will have to settle for the ordinary."

– Jim Rohn

Pratt, Parsons, RIT, Stanford, Georgia Tech, Carnegie Mellon, and RISD are six of the colleges that stand out for Industrial Design with amazing faculty, excellent facilities, and relatively easy access to internships. While most students consider New York City, Los Angeles, and San Francisco for the top college art programs and internships, they should not discount other major metropolitan areas like Chicago, Atlanta, Boston, Seattle, and Philadelphia as well as cities around the country that are meccas for design and manufacturing. However, you cannot go wrong going to Purdue for its deep dive into the world of engineering design. These colleges offer a rigorous course of study and socially responsible projects on the cutting edge of innovation, design, engineering, and forward-thinking optimism.

FINANCIAL AID

Nearly every university in the United States offers money for college. These funds come in the form of grants/scholarships that do not need to be paid back, loans that need to be repaid, and 'work study', where you are paid for a job associated with the college or university. The grants or scholarships are either need-based or merit-based. Need-based means that the college or government determines that, based on your income, you will be unable to attend without additional resources. Merit-based means that the college or university is offering you money based on some combination of your grades, test scores, skills, and/or talent.

To obtain need-based financial aid, almost all colleges require you to submit the Free Application for Federal Student Aid (FAFSA) found at www.studentaid.gov.

Some colleges also require the College Scholarship Service (CSS) Profile which is available on the College Board website at www.collegeboard.org.

Both the FAFSA and CSS Profile require you to submit your income based upon the tax returns you and/or your family file with the U.S. federal government.

If your answer is yes to any of the following you do not need to declare your parent's income when filing your FAFSA form. There are nuances to this for students who are verifiably independent, ex-pats that have a unique situation, and parents who are unavailable for a variety of reasons. The federal government offers advising if you have a unique case.

1. Will you be 24 or older by Jan. 1 of the school year for which you are applying for financial aid? For example, if you plan to start school in August 2022 for the 2022–23 school year, will you be 24 by Jan. 1, 2022 (i.e., were you born before Jan. 1, 1999)?

2. Are you married or separated but not divorced?

3. Will you be working toward a master's or doctorate degree (such as MA, MBA, MD, JD, Ph.D., Ed.D., etc.)?

4. Do you have children who receive more than half of their support from you?

5. Do you have dependents (other than children or a spouse) who live with you and receive more than half of their support from you?

6. Are you currently serving on active duty in the U.S. armed forces for purposes other than training?

7. Are you a veteran of the U.S. armed forces?

8. At any time since you turned age 13, were both of your parents deceased, were you in foster care, or were you a ward or dependent of the court?

9. Are you an emancipated minor or are you in a legal guardianship as determined by a court?

10. Are you an unaccompanied youth who is homeless or self-supporting and at risk of being homeless?

Most people will be able to download the tax information directly into the FAFSA form using the Data Retrieval Tool (DRT). This automatic process not only saves time, but the DRT also ensures that the correct information goes into the right locations on the form. Check anyway afterward since there could be an error. If your family has not filed a tax return yet, you may estimate the amounts. However, all income and other financial information will eventually need to be verified for you to receive need-based aid.

SCHOLARSHIPS

Merit scholarships are often offered through a college or university. These are based upon academic success, talent, or life experiences. These may not have additional forms and essays to complete. Merit scholarships based upon talent typically require a portfolio, performance, audition, or some other demonstration of your skills. Check your art, dance, music, writing, theatre, research, robotics, engineering, or program to see what the college requires. Note: Each college or university has a different set of rules for what and how you submit your art, video, writing samples, or other demonstration of your mastery.

Please check out the profile section at the back of this book for scholarships and requirements. Additionally, look up the college website for their financial aid process. To help you get a sense of available scholarships, I selected four schools from the options listed in the profile section.

Pratt Institute

Pratt offers generous merit-based scholarships. Sixty percent of incoming first-year students are offered merit-based awards for their talent. In addition, Pratt has restricted and endowed scholarships along with its need-based financial aid program. International students are also eligible for merit-based awards. No additional application is required for prospective students; all admitted students are considered automatically.

Rhode Island School of Design

RISD offers scholarships to students who demonstrate academic and talent-based success and financial need. Many students receive $20,000 awards. However, scholarships are need-based, and international students must pay the full tuition.

Savannah College of Art and Design (SCAD)

Some colleges are exceptionally generous with money for a large proportion of students. For example, at SCAD, 80% of new applicants receive merit & need-based scholarships. These opportunities are available for U.S. citizens, permanent residents, and international students.

Syracuse University

Syracuse University students received more than $400 million in financial aid. Syracuse offers internal merit-based scholarships and supports students in finding external funds as well. Merit-based funding is offered to more than 35% of the incoming class. Approximately 80% of SU's incoming students received some type of financial support. Syracuse University offers a financial aid package to incoming students that meet full-need.

PRIVATE SCHOLARSHIPS

Some scholarship money does not come directly from the college. Private individuals, corporations, and endowments offer outside scholarships for students who apply. Some of these scholarships are significant. A few offer full tuition. Here are a few of the thousands to consider.

AQHA and AQHF – $25,000 - $35,000 (Dec 1) Quarter Horse Members

A few scholarships for journalism, communications, agricultural studies, and equine research.

Boren Scholarships ($8,000 - $25,000) and Boren Fellowships ($12,000 -30,000) – Foreign Language Study

The National Security Education Program (NSEP) awards funding for students to study one of about 65 languages the U.S. deems necessary for national security through a study abroad program. Applications open from mid-August to early February. Approximately 300 student selected.

Brower Youth Awards

Environmental activism awards are granted to 6 winners; each receives $3,000.

Coca Cola Scholarship

1,400 students are selected to receive scholarships. The total amount awarded annually is approximately $3,550,000. 150 students receive $20,000 scholarship each.

Comcast NBCUniversal Leaders and Achievers Scholarship

More than 800 high school student winners each year win a $2,500 scholarship.

Dell Scholars Program – 500 students selected – $20,000 - First-Generation

This scholarship is awarded to students who exhibit grit, potential, and ambition.

Distinguished Scholars Awards, Art Contest Scholarships

There are numerous scholarships that fall into these categories.

Gates Millennium Scholarship

Scholarships covering the full cost of attendance not already covered by other aid and expected family contributions are granted to 300 African American, American Indian/Alaska Native, Asian Pacific Islander, or Hispanic American student leaders.

GE-Reagan Foundation Scholarship Program $40,000 (10 students)

Another $50,000 is awarded in the Great Communicator Debate Series.

Gloria Barron Prize for Young Heroes

25 students each year ages 8 – 18 receive $10,000 for community service projects.

Hispanic Scholarship Fund

Approximately 10,000 winners - $30,000,000 awarded annually.

K-12 Educator Scholarship

This scholarship is for children with parents who teach in the K-12 system.

NAACP – National Association for the Advancement of Colored People

African Americans - about 170 students receive awards of $3,000 to $15,000.

NASSP – National Association of Secondary School Principals

600 NHS Scholarships awarded per year, 1 national winner ($25,000 scholarship). 24 national finalists ($5,625 each), 575 national semifinalists ($3,200 each). Apply between October 1 and December 1.

Parent Employment

Many companies offer scholarships for their employees and their children.

Prudential Spirit of Community Award (Prudential Emerging Visionaries)

25 students in grades 5 to 12 are granted a $1,000 - $5,000 award for community service.

Questbridge Scholarship

$200,000 is granted to each of 1,464 students to be used over 4 years.

ROTC

These military scholarships are not given to everyone in ROTC. A select group of outstanding candidates is given tuition, fees, textbooks, plus a monthly stipend.

Scholastic Art and Writing Competition

Herblock Award - $1,000 scholarships for editorial cartoons

New York Life Award - $1,000 writing award about personal grief and loss

One Earth Award - $1,000 scholarship for writing about human-caused climate change

Portfolio Scholarships – Up to $10,000 granted for top portfolios

Civic Expression Award - $1,000 scholarships for writing on political and social issues

Best-In-Grade – Juror favorite awards receive $500 scholarships

College Tuition & Summer Scholarships - https://www.artandwriting.org/scholarships/

Service/Leadership/Focused Organization Scholarship

Lions Club, Moose Club, Elks Club, Rotary Club, Soroptimists Club, Mensa

Target Scholarship

HBCU Design Challenge for African Americans – Students submit designs for Black History Month.

Target Scholars Program – 1,000 students get $5,000 each.

Thurgood Marshall College Fund

African Americans – approximately 500 scholarships per year (average award - $6,200 per year).

CHAPTER 10

SUPPLEMENTAL MATERIALS AND PORTFOLIOS FOR INDUSTRIAL & PRODUCT DESIGN PROGRAMS

"The way I see it, if you want the rainbow, you gotta put up with the rain."

– Dolly Parton

At the top Industrial Design schools like Rhode Island School of Design, Carnegie Mellon, Stanford, Georgia Tech, Rochester Institute of Technology, and the University of Michigan, acceptance is very difficult. Furthermore, the BFA, BDes, and BID degrees are completely immersive. Inspired by the environment, you will be surrounded by students who are creative, multitalented, and focused.

Students must be wholly dedicated to design. Thus, admissions officers are keenly interested in the applicant's talent and commitment. As a result, a portfolio review is required for the top schools; sometimes, an interview is part of the admissions process as well. Applicants must demonstrate ability and potential.

CHANGES IN THE APPLICANT DEMOGRAPHICS CHALLENGES ON THE ROAD AHEAD

COVID-19 shook students as well as admissions offices. Many studio-centered programs closed down or went online. International students left for their country of origin and classes at a distance could not provide the needed materials, space, and opportunities. Many quit and did not return.

Furthermore, some design programs completely shut down. Colleges faced a crisis. While some programs reopened after COVID-19 and some students returned, demographic shift s resulted, including gender diversity and ethnic makeup. Check the colleges again for the programs you want. Additionally, international students hesitated to apply which shook design programs. Nevertheless, many returned.

Other challenges existed as well. COVID-19 changed the makeup of applicants to college. Many students of color chose not to apply. Other data show that while enrollments rebounded, some programs suffered from budget cuts.

NATIONAL PORTFOLIO DAYS

These online and in-person national events are free for students to participate anywhere they are located in the world. In-person events are often held both inside and outside of the United States. Prospective art program applicants have the chance to meet admissions staff and present art pieces. Students must register online. There are filters with the online registration so you can sign up for events that fit your needs: online in-person, undergraduates, transfer, or graduate school.

In-person events can be jam-packed with people, though COVID-19 changed procedures with limited numbers of individuals inside venues. In the past, massive lines where students waited for their turn sometimes resulted in disappointed latecomers. In some locations, now, there is a reservation system. Make sure you read about any required protocols for in-person events.

More than fifty colleges come to many of the in-person events. Typically, you will have 10 to 15 minutes to speak to a representative and show them your work. You should bring a range of pieces. The website recommends bringing 10 – 12 pieces. Even if you only bring five, you are fine. The point is for your work to be reviewed so you can gain valuable feedback and improve.

For the online events, there are live sessions where you wait in a 'waiting room' queue until you can be seen. You can also schedule a meeting, though only on the day of the event. You may register for multiple school reviews. Note that you will not upload your portfolio. Rather, you will meet with your reviewer via Zoom and share your screen.

These events do not guarantee admission, and no admissions decisions are made at these events. In addition, although the colleges may suggest that you apply for their scholarships or be considered for their merit awards, you will not be awarded any money at these events.

In most cases, you will still need to present your portfolio online through the school-determined application portal. Even so, these events are excellent in that they allow you to meet people from various colleges and they get a chance to meet you. Furthermore, you get helpful advice and suggestions on how you can improve the pieces you plan to submit.

PORTFOLIO REQUIREMENTS

Portfolios are required for a few Industrial Design programs. Since students often apply to 10-20 schools, the effort can be daunting. Furthermore, completing applications and creating portfolios take time and money. Costs include training, preparation, application fees, and other expenses. For some schools, there are fee waivers.

The first entry point to Industrial Design programs is investigating colleges. Apply to your dream school, but also select colleges that have programs that fit your criteria – classes, program requirements, geography, studio space, faculty, career prospects, cost, etc. For now, let's look at the portfolio requirements at a few schools. Start by getting a general idea of what each school requires so that you are prepared. More information is provided in the profiles later on in this book.

CARNEGIE MELLON UNIVERSTIY

BDes (Bachelor of Design) – Products
BDes (Bachelor of Design) – Environments
MDes (Master of Design); MA in Design

CMU's School of Design requests a video, portfolio, and essay posted to SlideRoom. The 90 second or less video should convey your authentic passion, interests outside of school and an experience that changed you. You may use your phone. No editing software is required. Your portfolio should represent a wide range of creative skills with finished and process work. You will submit no more than 18 pieces.

You may submit 2-D, 3-D, and 4-D work that display and describe your creative process. You may show your sketchbook, journal, or notebook. Include at least one slide that shows how you think and visualize ideas. You are encouraged to submit drawings but may also send in mixed media, sculpture, photography, or animated digital representations.

You will also submit a 250-500-word essay. CMU requests that you choose something in your neighborhood that requires a significant change. This can be an object, situation, process, or an emergent issue. Provide a critique as well as your ideas as to how your design can have a positive impact.

GEORGIA INSTITUTE OF TECHNOLOGY

BS Industrial Design
MFA Industrial Design

Georgia Tech does not require a portfolio, but they do allow students to submit one. The admissions committee would like to gain a deeper insight into your visual training, professional aspirations, and unique qualifications for their Industrial Design program. Freshman are given a link the Design Portfolio on the portal where you receive your application status updates. You must submit by the due date EA or RD.

Submit 10 or fewer high-quality reproductions of your best and most recent artwork. Tech is looking for original work rather than copied art pieces. You may submit real-life observational drawings, paintings, 2-D/3-D design, photography, woodworking, sculpture, or other visual media. Label each with the size, medium, assigned, and a couple of sentences of an explanation.

KEAN UNIVERSITY

BS Industrial Design

Portfolios are required for the Michael Graves College. You may apply through the CommonApp or the Kean University application. After you submit your application, you will receive instructions as to how to upload your portfolio.

Applicants are expected to be prepared for the rigorous program and demonstrate their talent by submitting 10-12 pieces for review. Select your best work, displaying your creative thinking in a variety of media or subject matter. You will be evaluated based on visualization, visual form, technical abilities, creativity, presentation, and professionalism.

UNIVERSITY OF NOTRE DAME

BA Industrial Design
BFA Industrial Design
MFA Industrial Design

A portfolio is not required but highly recommended.

PARSONS SCHOOL OF ART AND DESIGN

BFA Product Design
MFA Industrial Design

Parsons requests an uploaded portfolio of eight to twelve images from a student's breadth of media skills, including drawing, painting, sculpture, design, collage, animation, etc. Experimentation, imagination, and self-expression are key. Include documentation and descriptions of your work and process. Parsons also requires a submission called "The Parsons Challenge". Start this part early. Many students put this off, and either do a lackluster job or cannot pull this together before the deadline. The Parsons Challenge is a new visual work inspired by a theme expressed in work within the portfolio. Students submit a required 500-word essay describing the development of the idea. Two additional pieces may be added to document your process. Observational work is not required since technique and vision are emphasized in the review.

PURDUE UNIVERSITY

BFA Industrial Design
MFA Industrial Design

A portfolio is not required. Nevertheless, students must pass a required and selective portfolio review during the spring of their sophomore year.

RHODE ISLAND SCHOOL OF DESIGN

BFA Industrial Design
MID (Master of Industrial Design)

After completing the Common Application, students will submit a SlideRoom supplement. Students present 12-20 of their recent work on the SlideRoom site. RISD requests finished pieces, drawings from direct observation, and no more than three pieces that show research and prep work. RISD's admissions are competitive, so you should curate and edit the pieces you choose to submit in your portfolio.

RISD offers its own portfolio days online, where they will review your work and give you a valuable critique. Hint: RISD looks for engaged learners who will connect with the world. They want art that says something meaningful, evokes emotion and shares a point of view. Being technically strong is essential but being emotionally strong and inextricably linked to the audience is imperative. Thus, more is not better. Only share your best work.

STANFORD UNIVERSITY

BS Engineering - Product Design
MS Engineering – Product Design

A portfolio is not required. However, if you have extraordinary talent or have received awards for your work, you may submit an Arts Portfolio by responding "Yes" on the CommonApp or CoalitionApp.

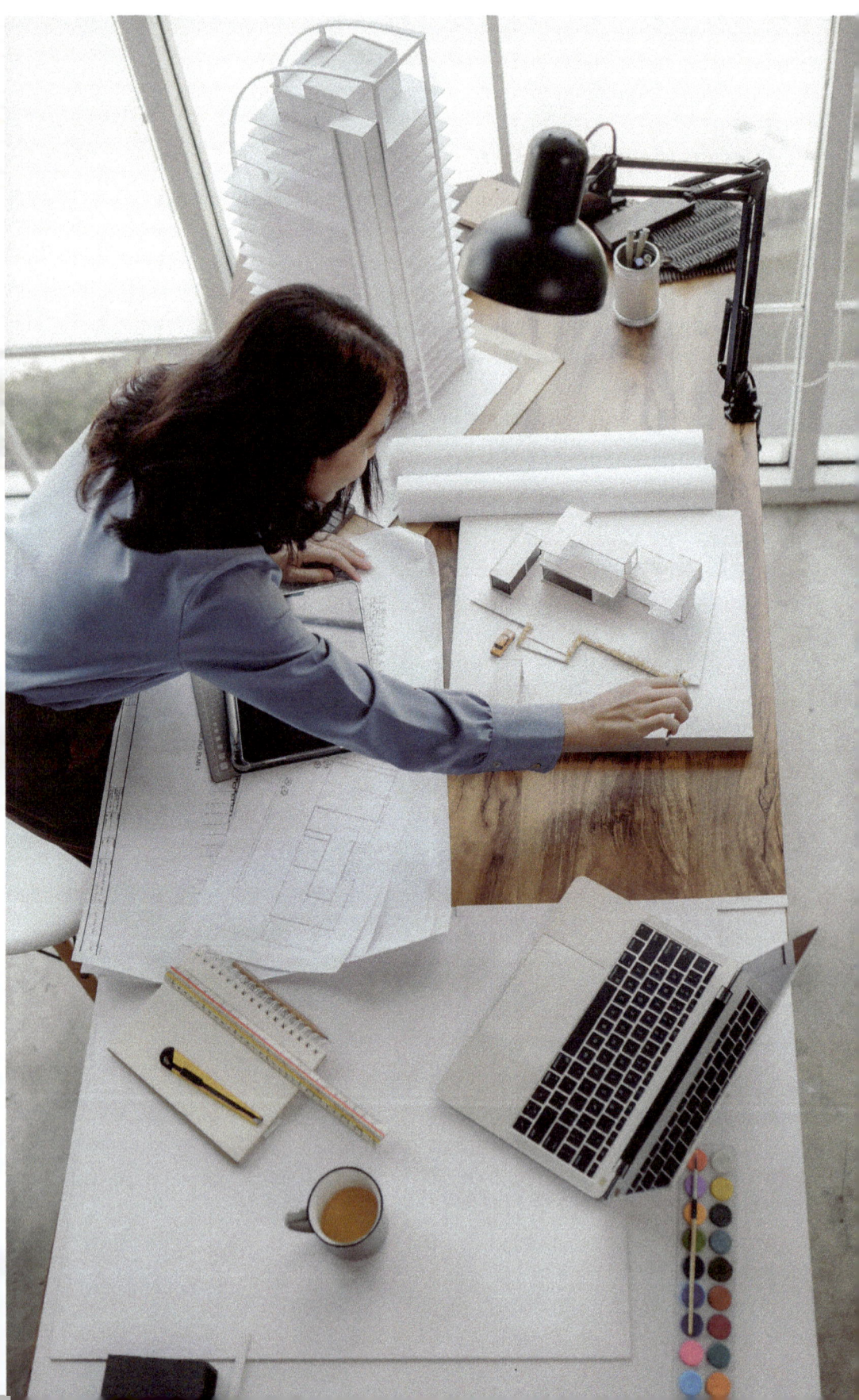

CHAPTER 11

POST PANDEMIC EMPLOYMENT OUTLOOK: STATISTICS AND ECONOMIC PROJECTIONS

"You are the sky. Everything else is just the weather."

– Pema Chödrön

ndustrial Designers enter many different fields and play essential roles in society. According to the *Occupational Outlook Handbook*, employment opportunities in these fields are slated to grow from 2020 to 2030 at different rates with new jobs expected. The median annual wage for entry-level positions is given below. The job outlook for artists is good with a 14% growth rate. Wages are also likely to increase.

According to the 2022 Bureau of Labor Statistics,[1]

OCCUPATION	JOB SUMMARY	ENTRY-LEVEL EDUCATION	MEDIAN PAY
Advertising Sales and Agents	Advertising sales agents sell advertising space to businesses and individuals.	High School Diploma or Equivalent	$52,340
Archivists, Curators, and Museum Workers	Archivists and curators oversee institutions' collections, such as historical items or of artwork. Museum technicians and conservators prepare and restore items in those collections.	Varies	$50,120
Art Directors	Art directors are responsible for the visual style and images in magazines, newspapers, product packaging, and movie and television productions.	Bachelor's Degree	$100,890
Broadcast, Sound, and Video Technicians	Broadcast, sound, and video technicians set up, operate, and maintain the electrical equipment for media programs.	Varies	$49,050
Craft and Fine Artists	Craft and fine artists use a variety of materials and techniques to create art for sale and exhibition.	Varies	$49,960
Dancers and Choreographers	Dancers and choreographers use dance performances to express ideas and stories.	Varies	N/A
Desktop Publishers	Desktop publishers use computer software to design page layouts for items that are printed or published online.	Associate's Degree	$46,910
Editors	Editors plan, review, and revise content for publication.	Bachelor's Degree	$63,350
Fashion Designers	Fashion designers create clothing, accessories, and footwear.	Bachelor's Degree	$77,450

---

1   Bureau of Labor Statistics, U.S. Department of Labor, *Occupational Outlook Handbook*, Craft and Fine Artists, at https://www.bls.gov/ooh/arts-and-design/craft-and-fine-artists.htm.

OCCUPATION	JOB SUMMARY	ENTRY-LEVEL EDUCATION	MEDIAN PAY
Film and Video Editors & Camera Operators	Film and video editors and camera operators manipulate moving images that entertain or inform an audience.	Bachelor's Degree	$60,360
Graphic Designers	Graphic designers create visual concepts, using computer software or by hand, to communicate ideas that inspire, inform, and captivate consumers.	Bachelor's Degree	$50,710
Industrial Designers	Industrial designers combine art, business, and engineering to develop the concepts for manufactured products.	Bachelor's Degree	$77,030
Jewelers & Precious Stone & Metal Workers	Jewelers and precious stone and metal workers design, construct, adjust, repair, appraise and sell jewelry.	Bachelor's Degree	$46,640
Market Research Analysts	Market research analysts study market conditions to examine potential sales of a product or service.	Bachelor's Degree	$63,920
News Analysts, Reporters, and Journalists	News analysts, reporters, and journalists keep the public updated about current events and noteworthy information.	Bachelor's Degree	$48,370
Postsecondary Teachers	Postsecondary teachers instruct students in a variety of academic subjects beyond the high school level.	Master's Degree	$79,640
Producers and Directors	Producers and directors make business and creative decisions about film, television, stage, and other productions.	Bachelor's Degree	$79,000
Public Relations & Fundraising Managers	Public relations managers direct the creation of materials that will enhance the public image of their employer or client. Fundraising managers coordinate campaigns that bring in donations for their organization.	Bachelor's Degree	$119,860
Public Relations Specialists	Public relations specialists create and maintain a positive public image for the clients they represent.	Bachelor's Degree	$62,800

OCCUPATION	JOB SUMMARY	ENTRY-LEVEL EDUCATION	MEDIAN PAY
Sales Managers	Sales managers direct organizations' sales teams.	Bachelor's Degree	$127,490
Photographers	Photographers use their technical expertise, creativity, and composition skills to produce and preserve images.	Bachelor's Degree	$38,950
Special Effects Artists & Animators	Special effects artists and animators create images that appear to move and visual effects for various forms of media and entertainment.	Bachelor's Degree	$78,790
Technical Writers	Technical writers prepare instruction manuals, how-to guides, journal articles, and other supporting documents to communicate complex and technical information more easily.	Bachelor's Degree	$78,060
Woodworkers	Woodworkers manufacture a variety of products, such as cabinets and furniture, using wood, veneers, and laminates.	High School Diploma or Equivalent	$36,710
Writers and Authors	Writers and authors develop written content for various types of media.	Bachelor's Degree	$67,120

We know what we are but know not what we may be.

– William Shakespeare

Industrial Designers work in studios where they immortalize ideas in a job that is a cross between designer, Imagineer, and engineer. Industrial Designers occasionally travel to testing and manufacturing facilities, design centers, client's facilities., and exhibitions/conferences.

The median pay for an Industrial Designer is $77,030 with a bachelor's degree. Those with a master's degree are typically paid higher due to their more specialized, focused knowledge. The employment prospects for designers are positive with 6% growth and approximately 3,100 new jobs expected each year for the next decade.

Similar jobs, listed in the previous chart, vary across subjects since designers have different focuses. The fluidity and opportunity in Industrial Design work spans across toy design, furnishings, household items, vehicles, and business. Skills also vary, including marketing, manufacturing, and leadership. Society has a wide and varied use for the skills of an Industrial Designer. However, you will need to discover your personal areas of interest.

The skills an Industrial Design student learns in school, including drawing, modeling, engineering, and computer-aided design, are valuable and transferrable to other fields as well. According to the Bureau of Labor Statistics, approximately 41% of artists work in manufacturing, while 12% work in wholesale trade, 10% in specialized design services, 7% in architectural, engineering, and related services, and 3% are self-employed.[2]

IMPACT OF COVID-19

COVID-19 impacted the number of jobs people could get in design. A significant drop in opportunities led most designers to the internet to post their portfolio and set up their independent work for freelancing. The dynamic changed as Pinterest, Instagram, and Facebook became inundated with images.

One of my friends in the publishing business said that freelancers needed a "megaphone" or "gimmick" to get noticed. He is not a gimmicky kind of guy, so he searches for platforms to broadcast his work. Thus, the impact of COVID-19 cannot be understated. While the field is booming with more entrants presenting what they created, practicing continues to be essential, and technique can always be improved.

Companies are back to hiring now and good jobs are available in Industrial Design. There is no doubt that the skills are tremendously valuable and multidimensional.

ROAD TO BECOMING A DESIGNER

The road to success in this industry should not be discouraging, although a few steps are required along the way. Even so, achieving the goal is rewarding. Encourage those around you. If this is the field you want to pursue, pave the road in front of you and drive.

An internship or apprenticeship or two in peripheral areas would not hurt you in your pursuit of gigs and contract work. Although some internships are unpaid,

---

2   Bureau of Labor Statistics, U.S. Department of Labor, *Occupational Outlook Handbook*, Craft and Fine Artists, at https://www.bls.gov/ooh/arts-and-design/craft-and-fine-artists.htm

you will find that most applicants will have one or more. Some internships pay fairly well. Even if you will ultimately be a freelancer, you might find parallel bread and butter professions while you fine-tune your craft.

If you are serious, you will make a fantastic career out of your pursuit. Initiative-taking persistence, talent, creativity, and moxie can get you into your desired college program and career. You may have to start at the very bottom of the ladder, but you can climb the rungs methodically one by one.

Companies want to know employees' work ethic, personality, and professionalism. An internship allows you to get to know the corporate climate better and allows others to get to know you better too. Thus, many companies hire the interns they feel are the best fit rather than choosing candidates from the piles of resumes that have been submitted.

Education unlocks doors no matter which direction your career takes you. Whatever direction you pursue, if you lay a foundation, undaunted by the competition, and are unafraid of starting at the bottom, you will do fine. Hard work and creativity go a long way in this industry. Start by getting a solid education.

MANAGEMENT AND EMPLOYEE RETENTION

Skills to Know: Management, Human Resources, Social Consciousness, Ethics

One of the most significant challenges facing employers in the years from 2022 - 2030 will be locating and retaining talent. The pandemic slowed education and learning with online classes, reduced access to faculty/advising, limited access to labs, inability to attend workshops, retail closures, and fewer conferences, meetings, and shows. Health concerns rose to the top of importance as did financial stress, job uncertainty, and social consciousness.

Many students chose to work rather than study and start online stores when they could not access locations for community service or continue with their sport, instrument, or hobbies. With the changes in lifestyle and fears about health, safety, and wellness, many bright and talented students developed a fearless sense of autonomy and independence, while for others, the necessary skills ordinarily developed in school were fraught by limitations.

Finding talent within the changing hiring atmosphere will require new skills. Employees are increasingly looking elsewhere for a better opportunity. This development will require managers to earn and harness employee trust and loyalty.

The digital workforce has also placed demands on human resources. While many companies want their employees to work in-person, the convenience of working at home and the drudgery of commuting to work have created an environment where employees seek greater flexibility. Changes are coming. The employee talent challenge is likely to create a more global workforce where companies look for less expensive online talent from a pool of eager workers in other countries.

CHAPTER 12

NEXT STEPS: PREPARATION AND REAL-WORLD SKILLS

"If you really want to do something, you'll find a way. If you don't, you'll find an excuse."

– Jim Rohn

Collage offers you the freedom to express yourself openly, dynamically, and interactively. As you explore Industrial and Product Design in society, you will engage the artistic side within you, hungry to emerge. The next step is for you to choose a college where your persona fits into the makeup of the environment. In college studios, you will receive personalized, interactive training, immersed and infused with inspiration from fellow classmates.

Each prototype you construct will leave a lasting impression. Through social media, instantaneously, you can share your inspirations, designs, and portfolio with millions of people in a matter of moments. The possibilities are limitless. In school or out of school, you may want to take a few classes on social media dynamics and website editing. Furthermore, on the leading edge of the Metaverse, you can create opportunities that were never before possible. It's unbelievably thrilling.

Industrial Design is a dynamic, multidimensional world where you contribute to the dialogue. In some careers, repetitive tasks and uninspiring projects lead employees to loathe their jobs and tick off minutes until their day is done. Yet, your life will undoubtedly be different and ever-changing since the world around you will change from moment to moment. Over time, whichever area of Industrial Design becomes your focus, you will earn your way to a career of endless possibilities.

If you watched companies such as Sony and Samsung grow,
they focused first on features and then on Industrial Design,
which made their products look and feel better.

- Jefferson Han

American landscape painter, George Inness, shared, "The true use of art is, first, to cultivate the artist's own spiritual nature." Spend time thinking, even though time sometimes seems short. You may feel as if time slips through your fingers like sand in an hourglass. Resist the temptation to upload your designs before contemplating what you want to express. While social media opens doors to share your creations, truly magical works are created when time stands still, and you immerse yourself in a creative state.

Today is a precious moment. As you contemplate college choices and tomorrow's future, you will explore your passion, open doors you never expected, and discover opportunities that will tantalize and challenge you along the way. As such, you will capture a new, exciting, and eclectic way of life.

Attending a respected school can help you get noticed. Your next steps are aided by connections offered by professors, classmates, and alumni. Networking at events is also an excellent way to discover opportunities. Shows, displays, and contests in school, out of school, in the summer, or through social media can help you get noticed. Bring people into your world. Allow them to feel and interpret your designs in their unique way.

Throughout your varied experiences, you will meet other Industrial Designers who may recommend you to employers or inform you about open positions or contract opportunities, even some that are not publicly announced. In addition, many schools have a culminating event where you can put your best foot forward and showcase your work. Exposure to industry professionals will open new doors. Also, by interacting with people online or in-person you can maintain those connections.

Autonomy and freedom to choose the jobs you take by venturing out on your own may seem alluring, but freelancing may result in uncertainty or even career limitations. As a result, companies often choose seasoned professionals with work experience in other firms. However, there are ways to mitigate against the lean times of solo work. A few options include demonstrating mastery, producing amazing work, resolving client problems, aligning ideologies, and initially charging less. Despite challenges, put yourself out there.

You could wait for the phone to ring to be discovered. However, you should post ideas, articles, or availability regularly to professional sites. To be seen, you need to be out and about. Some individuals pine away, hoping to be selected and deciding which organization would be a perfect fit. Others decide that they only want to work at a specific firm or location. Still others determine that they will work for themselves and be their own boss. Yet, sometimes taking any position at the start is a steppingstone to your dream life, commitment to service, and opportunity to put your unique mark on society.

BOLD NETWORKING

Networking takes social skills and a bit of moxie. From elevator speeches and professional encounters to interviews and masterclasses, your job is to find a way to get your work in front of people and have them see your talent and your potential to contribute. You have something special and fresh ideas. Finally, there is a professional entity that will welcome your style, ingenuity, discipline, and impact.

How can you be recognized? Meet people; hand out your resume; give them your business card; ask for their business card; follow up; ask if you can call or meet them, even when approaching these professionals may seem uncomfortable. Stay in touch with people you meet, even if it is just happenstance or serendipity. Keep a log with each person's phone, e-mail, identifying information, and both date and location where you met. You never know when you will need it.

If you meet people professionally at a workshop, leadership event, or industry conference, even if you do not exchange information, you will recognize them at a

later date. They may recognize you at a future event too. Keep training. You should always seek ways to improve, irrespective of your experience. Lifelong learning improves your ability to maintain up-to-date skills and transition to new ventures. Furthermore, the outside world's perspective changes more quickly with social media's instant influences.

Though you should not take workshops just for the sake of meeting people, when you attend, be present in your quest to lead, serve, and envision. If your focus is not on your improvement or development, you may appear insincere in your intentions. However, workshops, conferences, and contests can allow others to see your purpose, vision, and talent.

Big-ticket training does not always mean better trainers or opportunities. Find time to visit museums, survey your surroundings, and notice cultural changes. While gathering new thoughts, remember humility and open-mindedness go a long way. Defer to the wise and listen. There is much you can learn.

STAY IN TOUCH

Do not annoy busy people, but you can keep in touch every couple of months. Communicating more frequently is overwhelming. However, life is long. People who grow with their craft transition fluidly through life's career phases. In Industrial Design, contacts are essential in all phases of your career. Also, do not be surprised. Many go-getters seeking to gain a coveted contract do the following:

1. Speak at Chamber of Commerce meetings.
2. Attend art, design, and software trade shows.
3. Gain a following on Instagram and Pinterest.
4. Write a newsletter and publish it on LinkedIn and other sources.
5. Link your work to Facebook, Twitter, Instagram, Pinterest, and other social media.
6. Enter in art contests.
7. Join professional associations.
8. Attend social gatherings of potential customers.
9. Keep in touch with your professors.
10. Stay involved with your alumni associations.

Friendships matter. Become lifelong colleagues by finding friends who share mutual interests and offer a sounding board or connections to new opportunities. People tend to stay in touch with "important" people. Note to self: Your contemporaries or peers are important people...although possibly not yet. As you form lists of contacts, you are likely to know these people throughout your career.

Be audacious while also being authentic. Networking can sometimes appear fake or forced as if you are going out on a hunt to find people for your own benefit. Worse, the act of networking can appear like stalking for those who incessantly attempt to connect.

The mental image of this type of 'networking' conjures the vision of people congregating at meetings. Friendships and the mutual support of allies can be enormously helpful, though 20,000 or even 200,000 followers on your website do not mean you are popular. However, you can have unexpected meaningful exchanges if you get out, meet people, and live life.

There are times when deeply moving, casual conversations in non-professional settings could also turn into connections. Do not lose touch with people or burn bridges along the way. This industry is not that big, especially whatever subspecialty you choose. You will continually see extraordinary talent. You never know. They may contact you to collaborate one day or meet for coffee at an event.

COLLEGE AND CAREER CENTERS

Although Industrial and Product Design programs often have internal connections to help you secure an internship or job, you might also speak to someone at your campus career center. They often have interesting and possibly different prospects you might not get elsewhere. In addition, there may be a specific career liaison for their Industrial Design programs. Connect with them for help in your search process. Besides, you might want a related job that utilizes your creative, design, problem-solving, and presentation skills.

Career center coordinators often have excellent ideas of alternative options you may have never considered. Furthermore, they can assist you with creating a professional resume and cover letters for specific industries that are different from the ones you have for Industrial Design.

They may also connect you with past graduates in the industry who make excellent connections. Some of them may have been in your program and have been through the ropes, know a few people, and may be able to get you an interview or invite you to an industry event. Any contact may help you get your foot in the door or find a job to make money in the meantime.

LINKEDIN

LinkedIn is especially helpful for career searches. You can find numerous influential contacts on LinkedIn. After interviews or events, connect with each person you met on LinkedIn. Keep a contact list of individuals you get to know in your area of interest. Do not constantly try to connect with people you do not really know. However, if you have made the connection, occasionally keep in touch.

While some LinkedIn message boxes may be full and you may not get a reply, you can try. Some people have tens of thousands of LinkedIn followers. I have about 20,000 'contacts', which does not necessitate that I am important. Remember that a paycheck or lots of friends does not make you more worthy or successful. Worth and value emanate from within your heart. Occasionally, you hit on a lucky break. Though I do not have time to communicate with everyone, I have connected with some of my most inspiring authors, advisors, and intellectual leaders through LinkedIn.

FINALLY

Most people are willing to help you. Five percent will not. Thus, you have a 19 out of 20 chance of interacting with decent people who have the time and will give you advice. Don't lose faith in humanity just because you run into a few people who are too busy to stop for you or are too self-absorbed that they cannot answer your question.

Remember that talent is only the beginning. You need to sell yourself. As you organize your goals and responsibilities, remember to think one step ahead of where you want to be by making a game plan. Since actions speak louder than words, take action without complaining and spread kindness along the way. Burned bridges are tough to reconstruct.

Honesty and trustworthiness are worth more than any physical object. Earn this by working hard, being efficient, and telling the truth. Professionalism in your words and deeds is essential. Put away all distractions and focus on your tasks. Texts and social media take a surprising amount of time. Every action you take is a steppingstone to your future. Discipline is achieved by creating a goal and making it happen.

A nice note, card, or gift reminds people you are thinking about them, even when you are incredibly busy. Good friends who have your best interest may know doors that are not yet open for you. Keep in touch with them.

So, go on a walk, meet people, and live fully. Serendipity happens when you live life. However, your education is immensely valuable. Success happens when preparation meets opportunity. Thus, preparation is the best way to generate luck. Finally, even the most disciplined person can be lazy or inefficient. Fight this. Stay active. Make your life happen for you. Here are a few things to remember as you go out to pursue your dreams.

- Work ethic is everything.
- Excellence is expected.
- Learn what you do not know on your own time.
- Come to work prepared.
- Take constructive criticism well.
- Be respectful and courteous.
- Keep your cool under pressure.
- Avoid being timid.
- Stay on task.
- Come early.
- Stay late.
- Take your work seriously.
- Do more than expected.
- Be thoughtful and respectful.
- Read your e-mail/texts after hours in case something is important.
- Ask questions. No question is too stupid.
- Maintain a clean workspace.
- Dress and act professionally.
- Don't gossip or complain.
- Play when you are done.
- Avoid frustrating your phenomenally busy supervisor.
- Be straightforward, and don't beat around the bush.

You've Got This!

Be yourself; everyone else is already taken.

- Oscar Wilde

4
Regions

41
Programs

COLLEGE PROFILES AND REQUIREMENTS

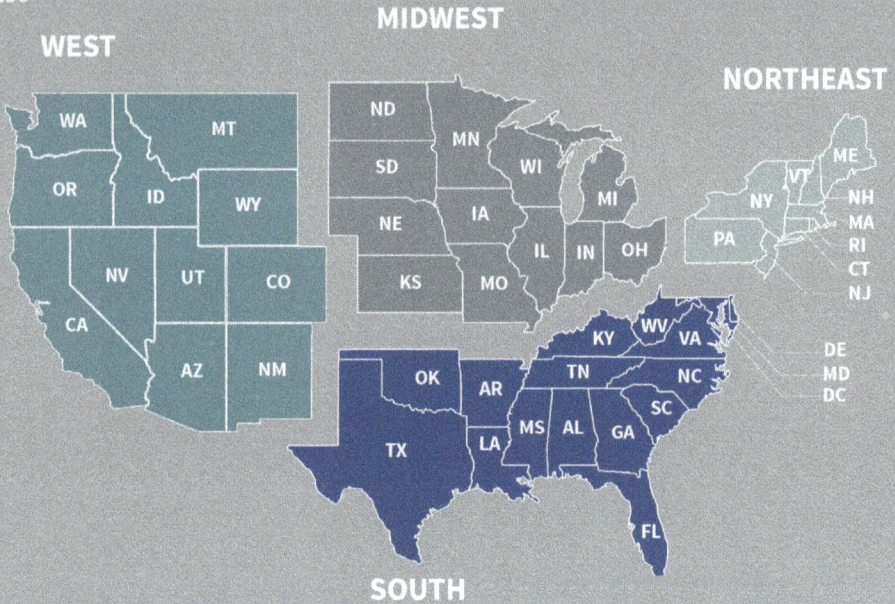

WEST · MIDWEST · NORTHEAST · SOUTH

PROGRAMS BY REGION
U.S. CENSUS BUREAU CLASSIFICATIONS

REGION 1 – NORTHEAST

Connecticut, Maine, Massachusetts, New Hampshire, New Jersey, New York, Pennsylvania, Rhode Island, and Vermont

REGION 2 – MIDWEST

Illinois, Indiana, Iowa, Kansas, Michigan, Minnesota, Missouri, Nebraska, North Dakota, Ohio, South Dakota, and Wisconsin

REGION 3 – SOUTH

Alabama, Arkansas, Delaware, District of Columbia, Florida, Georgia, Kentucky, Louisiana, Maryland, Mississippi, North Carolina, Oklahoma, South Carolina, Tennessee, Texas, Virginia, and West Virginia

REGION 4 – WEST

Alaska, Arizona, California, Colorado, Hawaii, Idaho, Montana, Nevada, New Mexico, Oregon, Utah, Washington, and Wyoming

LIST OF INDUSTRIAL & PRODUCT DESIGN PROGRAMS

The 41 programs listed in the following pages include profiles of the top undergraduate Industrial and Product Design programs as of April 2022 along with a few additional college programs that offer closely related degrees. Many students interested in studying Industrial and Product Design are often also interested in 3D design, graphic art, engineering, and architecture. Those schools are profiled in other books, though some lists are provided in the back.

Majoring in Industrial and Product Design is not for everyone. Although immensely rewarding, success requires passion, interest, and initiative. In college, students discover their priorities, commitments, and perseverance. A few choose an alternative path somewhere down the road.

Thus, this book provides you with lists of other programs so you can also explore those options. Keep the book handy. Even after you begin college you may find that the summer internships and alternative college programs are helpful.

Creating lists is often tedious and cumbersome. These lists were gathered to help you with this task. Descriptions of the college programs, tuition, requirements, and deadlines are accurate as of April 2022.

However, the requirements may have changed by the time you purchase this book. Nevertheless, this information is a great place to start!

Note: To simplify the text and fit information into the charts and descriptions, abbreviations were used as well as shortened sentences and acronyms.

CONNECTICUT

MAINE

MASSACHUSETTS

NEW HAMPSHIRE

NEW JERSEY

NEW YORK

PENNSYLVANIA

RHODE ISLAND

VERMONT

CHAPTER 13

REGION ONE

NORTHEAST

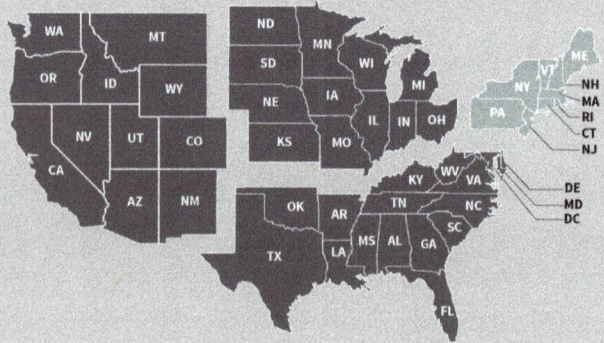

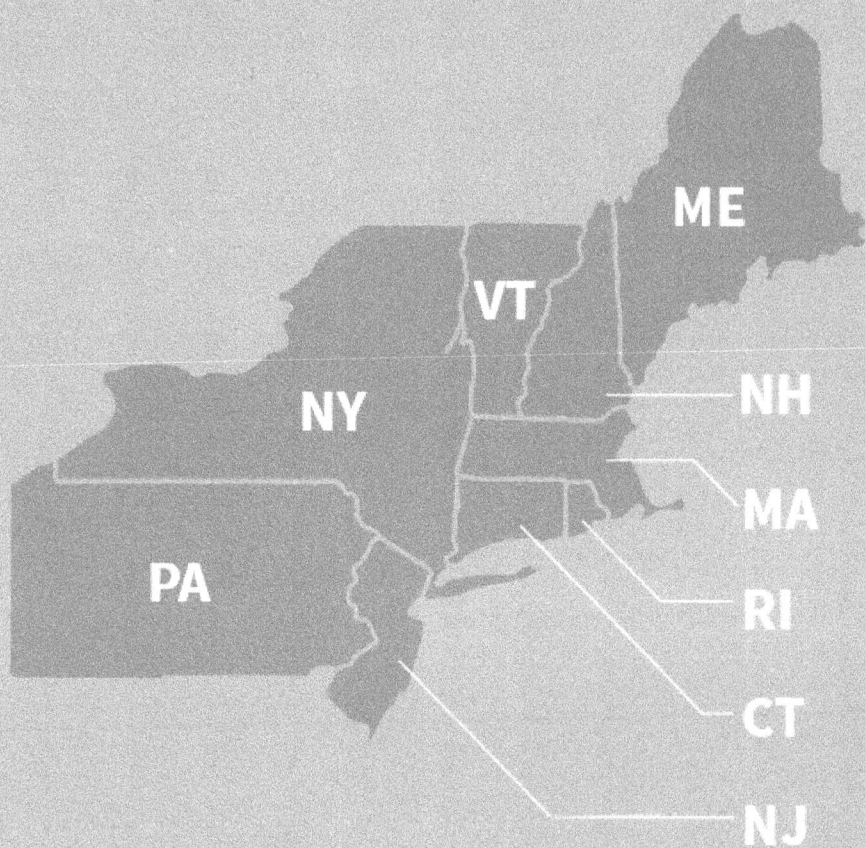

11 *Programs* | 9 *States*

INDUSTRIAL DESIGN PROGRAMS

School	Avg. GPA, SAT Evidence-Based Reading Writing (ERW), SAT Math (M), and ACT Composite (C) Early Decision (ED): Yes/No	Admission Statistics	Program(s)
Massachusetts College of Art & Design 621 Huntington Ave, Boston, MA 02115	GPA: N/A SAT (ERW): N/A SAT (M): N/A ACT (C): N/A *Test-optional ED: No	Admit Rate: 70% Undergrad Enrollment: 1,770 Total Enrollment: 1,894	BFA Industrial Design
Wentworth Institute of Technology 550 Huntington Ave, Boston, MA 02115	GPA: N/A SAT (ERW): 540-630 SAT (M): 550-650 ACT (C): 23-28 ED: No	Overall College Admit Rate: 94% Undergrad Enrollment: 4,222 Total Enrollment: 4,389	BS Industrial Design
Kean University 1000 Morris Ave, Union, NJ 07083	GPA: N/A SAT (ERW): 460-550 SAT (M): 460-550 ACT (C): 16-22 ED: No	Overall College Admit Rate: 78% Undergrad Enrollment: 11,686 Total Enrollment: 14,064	BS Industrial Design
Montclair State University 1 Normal Ave., Montclair, NJ 07043	GPA: N/A SAT (ERW): 500-600 SAT (M): 510-610 ACT (C): 21-28 *Test-optional ED: No	Overall College Admit Rate: 86% Undergrad Enrollment: 16,093 Total Enrollment: 20,744	BFA Product Design
Parsons - The New School 66 Fifth Avenue, New York, NY 10011	GPA: N/A SAT (ERW): 580-680 SAT (M): 560-680 ACT (C): 26-30 ED: No	Admit Rate: 69% Undergrad Enrollment: 6,399 Total Enrollment: 9,047	BFA Product Design MFA Industrial Design

School	Avg. GPA, SAT Evidence-Based Reading Writing (ERW), SAT Math (M), and ACT Composite (C)	Admission Statistics	Program(s)
	Early Decision (ED): Yes/No		
Pratt Institute 200 Willoughby Avenue, Brooklyn, NY 11205	GPA: 3.82 SAT (ERW): 570-660 SAT (M): 550-680 ACT (C): 25-30 ED: No	Admit Rate: 66% Undergrad Enrollment: 3,122 Total Enrollment: 4,353	Bachelor of Industrial Design Masters in Industrial Design
Rochester Institute of Technology 1 Lomb Memorial Dr, Rochester, NY 14623	GPA: 3.7 SAT (ERW): 600-690 SAT (M): 620-730 ACT (C): 28-33 ED: No	Overall College Admit Rate: 74% Undergrad Enrollment: 13,142 Total Enrollment: 16,158	BFA Industrial Design MFA Industrial Design
Syracuse University 401 University Place, Syracuse, NY 13244-2130	GPA: 3.67 SAT (ERW): N/A SAT (M): N/A ACT (C): N/A ED: Yes	Overall College Admit Rate: 69% Undergrad Enrollment: 14,479 Total Enrollment: 21,322	Bachelor of Industrial Design
Carnegie Mellon University 5000 Forbes Avenue, Pittsburgh, PA 15213	GPA: 3.85 SAT (ERW): 700-760 SAT (M): 760-800 ACT (C): 33-35 ED: Yes	Overall College Admit Rate: 17% Undergrad Enrollment: 7,073 Total Enrollment: 14,189	Bachelor of Design, Products Bachelor of Design, Environments MDes (Master of Design) MA in Design

NORTHEAST

INDUSTRIAL DESIGN PROGRAMS

School	Avg. GPA, SAT Evidence-Based Reading Writing (ERW), SAT Math (M), and ACT Composite (C) Early Decision (ED): Yes/No	Admission Statistics	Program(s)
Drexel University 3250 Chestnut Street, MacAlister Hall, Suite 4020, Philadelphia, PA 19104	GPA: N/A SAT (ERW): 590-680 SAT (M): 590-700 ACT (C): 25-31 ED: No	Admit Rate: 77% Undergrad Enrollment: 14,616 Total Enrollment: 23,589	BS Product Design MS Interior Architecture & Design
Pennsylvania College of Technology One College Avenue, Williamsport, PA 17701	GPA: N/A SAT (ERW): N/A* SAT (M): N/A* ACT (C): N/A* *Test-optional ED: No	Overall College Admit Rate: N/A Undergrad Enrollment: 4,565 Total Enrollment: 4,565	BS Industrial Design BS Engineering Design Technology BS Plastics & Polymer Engineering Technology BS Welding & Fabrication Engineering Technology
Rhode Island School of Design (RISD) 2 College St, Providence, RI 02903	GPA: N/A SAT (ERW): 610-700 SAT (M): 640-770 ACT (C): 27-32 ED: Yes	Admit Rate: 27% Undergrad Enrollment: 1,736 Total Enrollment: 2,227	BFA Industrial Design Master of Industrial Design

MASSACHUSETTS COLLEGE OF ART & DESIGN

Address: Massachusetts College of Art & Design
621 Huntington Ave,
Boston, MA 02115
Website: *https://massart.edu/academics/programs/industrial-design*
Contact: *https://massart.edu/contactus*
Phone: (617) 879-7667
Email: janderson@massart.edu

COST OF ATTENDANCE:

Tuition & Fees: $39,800 | **Additional Expenses:** $15,700
Total: $55,500

Financial Aid: https://massart.edu/financial-aid

ADDITIONAL INFORMATION:

Available Degree(s)

- BFA Industrial Design

Scholarships Offered

Merit and transfer scholarships, as well specific Foundation awards.

Summer Programs, Co-ops, Internships

"MassArt encourages students to acquire internships to help prepare them for careers in the Creative Economy. Career Development's mission is to support you as you find and complete an internship for credit."

Special Opportunities, Facilities/Equipment

All students; sophomores, juniors and seniors, are provided studio spaces which comprises of; a desk with shelving and pin-up space, a stool, a rolling storage unit and power. The space allocation gets slightly larger as students progress in the program. MassArt Art Museum Exhibitions; Museum of Fine Arts, Boston closeby

Notable Alumni

Kate Dudgeon

WENTWORTH INSTITUTE OF TECHNOLOGY

Address: School of Architecture & Design,
Wentworth Institute of Technology,
550 Huntington Ave, Boston, MA 02115
Website: *https://wit.edu/learning/school-architecture-design/industrial-design-bs*
Contact: *https://wit.edu/about/contact-us*
Phone: (617) 989-4909
Email: cribbsj@wit.edu

COST OF ATTENDANCE:

Tuition & Fees: $39,408 | **Additional Expenses:** $19,635
Total: $59,043

Financial Aid: https://wit.edu/admissions/financial-aid

ADDITIONAL INFORMATION:

Available Degree(s)

- BS Industrial Design

Scholarships Offered

Wentworth offers various types of merit and need-based aid.
Approximately 80% of all students receive some form of aid from
Wentworth. Merit scholarships include the ACE Mentor Scholarship,
the Boston Resident Scholarship, FIRST Robotics, Mass STEM Hub
Project, and many others.

Summer Programs, Co-ops, Internships

A team of support staff help students to participate in co-op
programs through listed positions at design and technology firms,
construction companies, and public service organizations. Co-op
options are offered abroad as well.

Special Opportunities, Facilities/Equipment

Over 60 labs and studios available.

Notable Alumni

Luther Blount and Dean Kamen

CONNECTICUT

MAINE

MASSACHUSETTS

NEW HAMPSHIRE

NEW JERSEY

NEW YORK

PENNSYLVANIA

RHODE ISLAND

VERMONT

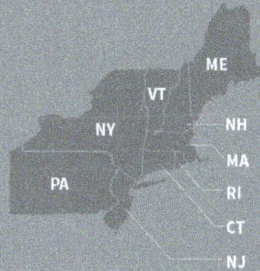

NORTHEAST

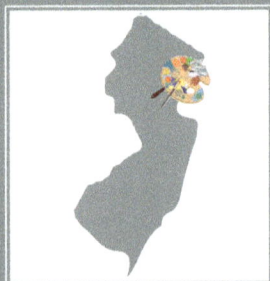

KEAN UNIVERSITY

Address: Robert Busch School of Design
Kean University
1000 Morris Ave
Union, NJ 07083
Website: *https://www.kean.edu/academics/programs/industrial-design*
Contact: *https://www.kean.edu/michaelgravescollege/faculty-staff*
Phone: (908) 737-4752
Email: rgonnell@kean.edu

COST OF ATTENDANCE:

Tuition & Fees: $19,771 | **Additional Expenses:** $18,115
Total: $37,886

Financial Aid: https://www.kean.edu/offices/financial-aid

ADDITIONAL INFORMATION:

Available Degree(s)

- BS Industrial Design

Portfolio Requirement

Upload to SlideRoom - 10-12 single file upload pieces and 400+ word essay. Portfolio evaluated on: visualization, visual form, technical, creativity, presentation, and professionalism

Scholarships Offered

Kean University offers merit-based and need-based aid to incoming students. The New Freshmen Merit Scholarships take into consideration standardized tests, academic rigor, course selection, class rank, and GPA. These scholarships are renewable for four years. Awards range from $4,000 to $50,000 per year.

Summer Programs, Co-ops, Internships

Students are given opportunities to pursue practical experience in their chosen field through internships, part-time employment, seminars and special events, including Kean's world-class Thinking Creatively Conference.

Special Opportunities, Facilities/Equipment

Michael Graves College Lecture Series, International Contemporary Furniture Fair, nonprofit collaboration including the still-in-development Mobile STEM Cabin project for Girl Scouts Heart of New Jersey.

Students from the industrial design program get the chance to present their work in 15-minute sessions with Aruliden industrial designers and receive immediate feedback to further develop their projects or presentations.

Notable Alumni

Tom Coyne and Alan R. Moon

CONNECTICUT

MAINE

MASSACHUSETTS

NEW HAMPSHIRE

NEW JERSEY

NEW YORK

PENNSYLVANIA

RHODE ISLAND

VERMONT

ME
VT
NY
NH
MA
PA
RI
CT
NJ

MONTCLAIR STATE UNIVERSITY

Address: Montclair State University
Calcia Hall, Suite 109
1 Normal Ave, Montclair, NJ 07043
Website: *https://www.montclair.edu/art-and-design/academic-programs/product-design-bfa/*
Contact: *https://www.montclair.edu/art-and-design/contact-us/*
Phone: (973) 655-7296
Email: feiglerd@montclair.edu

COST OF ATTENDANCE:

Tuition & Fees: $21,418 | **Additional Expenses:** $16,388
Total: $37,806

Financial Aid: https://www.montclair.edu/red-hawk-central/financial-aid/

ADDITIONAL INFORMATION:

Available Degree(s)

- BFA Product Design

Scholarships Offered

Major specific and institutional scholarships available.

Summer Programs, Co-ops, Internships

Dozens of internships available and required for the degree. As a product design major, you will work on real-life projects sponsored by manufacturing companies and design firms like Movado Group, Kaz Design and Ingersoll Rand, our esteemed industry partners.

You will then present your projects to senior designers, design directors, project managers and Brand VPs. Their invaluable feedback, based on professional expectations, will boost your awareness of industry-standards and, ultimately, your career preparation.

Special Opportunities, Facilities/Equipment

Study abroad with Mercedes Benz in Budapest and others with European companies engaged in design research and development. The Department of Art and Design occupies several buildings on campus. Its main facility is Calcia Halls. The BFA in Product Design program occupies the second floor of Finley Hall which includes a dedicated fabrication studio and lecture/workroom, as well as pecialized computer labs in the Sprague Library.

Notable Alumni

Jay Alders, Tobin Bell and A.J. Khubani

CONNECTICUT

MAINE

MASSACHUSETTS

NEW HAMPSHIRE

NEW JERSEY

NEW YORK

PENNSYLVANIA

RHODE ISLAND

VERMONT

NORTHEAST

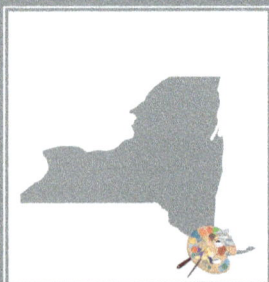

PARSONS SCHOOL OF DESIGN

Address: Parsons School of Design
66 Fifth Avenue, New York, NY 10011
Website: *https://www.newschool.edu/parsons/bfa-product-design/*
Contact: *https://www.newschool.edu/parsons/contact/*
Phone: (212) 229-8900
Email: thinkparsons@newschool.edu

COST OF ATTENDANCE:

Tuition & Fees: $54,546 | **Additional Expenses:** $27,550
Total: $82,096

Financial Aid: https://www.newschool.edu/parsons/financial-aid/

ADDITIONAL INFORMATION:

Available Degree(s)

- BFA Product Design
- MFA Industrial Design

Portfolio Requirement

Portfolios are required for incoming students. Applicants must complete the Parsons Challenge, a new visual work inspired by a theme set by the university. Applicants must also submit 8-12 works. Submit via SlideRoom.

Scholarships Offered

Scholarships available through Starfish.

Summer Programs, Co-ops, Internships

Our Career Services Office is enmeshed in the art and design industries and can help you advance your career with industry-oriented internships. Parsons offers online and on-campus summer programs for learners of all ages, from grades 3 through 12 to college students to working professionals.

Special Opportunities, Facilities/Equipment

Study Abroad program. Facilities include woodworking machinery, vacuum press equipment, CNC controlled milling machines, three-axis router/shaper table, machining lathes and mills, machinery for model-making with foams, plastics, and plastic vacuum forming, plastic casting, rubber mold making, painting, and finishing, MIG, TIG, ARC welding facilities, CNC plasma cutting,a nonferrous metal shop,a ceramic studio, which includes model making, mold making, and slip casting facilities, three oxidation kilns, and a glaze booth, PC workstations, 11x17" scanning, and 11x17" color laser printing capabilities, and a variety of 3D printers. In addition, product design students have access to a broad range of facilities including the SCE support facilities.

Notable Alumni

Bob Williams, Alina Roytberg, Hlynur Atlason,
Alex Lee, Emily Sugihara, Hinda Miller, and Christiane Lemieux.

CONNECTICUT

MAINE

MASSACHUSETTS

NEW HAMPSHIRE

NEW JERSEY

NEW YORK

PENNSYLVANIA

RHODE ISLAND

VERMONT

PRATT INSTITUTE

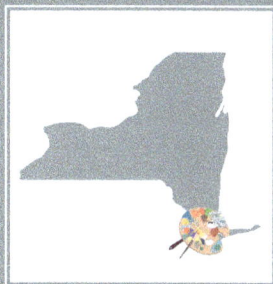

Address: Pratt Institute
Pratt Studios, Fourth Floor
200 Willoughby Avenue, Brooklyn, NY 11205
Website: *https://www.pratt.edu/academics/school-of-design/*
undergraduate-school-of-design/undergraduate-industrial-design/
Contact: *https://www.pratt.edu/academics/school-of-design/*
undergraduate-school-of-design/undergraduate-industrial-design/
industrial-design-office-contact/
Phone: (718) 636-3600
Email: id@pratt.edu

COST OF ATTENDANCE:

Tuition & Fees: $55,575 | **Additional Expenses:** $22,032
Total: $77,607

Financial Aid: https://www.pratt.edu/admissions/financing-your-education/

ADDITIONAL INFORMATION:

Available Degree(s)

- BID (Bachelor in Industrial Design)
- MID (Masters in Industrial Design)

Portfolio Required
Submit Common App before entering SlideRoom. Writing and visual
requirements include 12-20 pieces of artwork, including not copied/
replicated observational drawings in a variety of media (3-5 of these
must be from direct observation - landscape, still-life, self-portrait,
figure drawings, and interior spaces). Admissions reviews during
National Portfolio Days or by appointment off-campus do not fulfill
the applicant's visual requirement. They are for guidance only.

Scholarships Offered
Many institutional and private scholarships available.

Summer Programs, Co-ops, Internships
Internships available; study abroad at European design schools,
and a summer program in furniture making in Copenhagen through
the Danish International School.

Special Opportunities, Facilities/Equipment
The Industrial Design Shop provides the tools to fabricate both
small scale models or full size prototypes and functioning products.
Wood, plastics, dense foam, and metals are among the many types
of material that can be machined or manipulated. There is a Rapid
Prototyping Lab, photo studio, and down-draft tables and several
work tables for assembly/construction are available 24/7. The shop
houses a spray booth for exclusively water based paints/finishes.
During senior year students complete a capstone studio project,
presented at the annual Design Show, a public event attended by
industry leaders and potential employers.

Notable Alumni
William Boyer, Pres Bruning, Jason Freeny,
Donald Genaro, Pelle Petterson, Charles Pollock,
and Tony Schwartz

CONNECTICUT

MAINE

MASSACHUSETTS

NEW HAMPSHIRE

NEW JERSEY

NEW YORK

PENNSYLVANIA

RHODE ISLAND

VERMONT

NORTHEAST

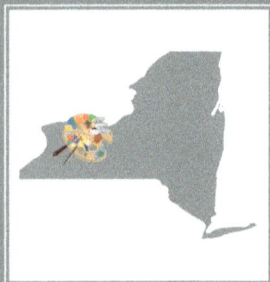

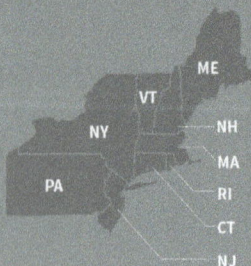

ROCHESTER INSTITUTE OF TECHNOLOGY

Address: Rochester Institute of Technology
College of Art and Design
55 Lomb Memorial Drive
Rochester, NY 14623
Website: *https://www.rit.edu/artdesign/industrial-design*
Contact: *https://www.rit.edu/artdesign/contact*
Phone: (505) 475-6152
Email: artdesign@rit.edu

COST OF ATTENDANCE:

Tuition & Fees: $69,496 | **Additional Expenses:** $2,858
Total: $72,354

Financial Aid: http://www.rit.edu/emcs/financialaid/

ADDITIONAL INFORMATION:

Available Degree(s)

- BFA Industrial Design
- MFA Industrial Design

Portfolio Required

Studio art experience and a portfolio of original artwork are required. RIT is looking for creativity and craftsmanship in the 10 -20 pieces you submit of your best artwork. There should be a minimum of three samples of drawings made from direct observation (not copied from photographs, comics, or "fantasy"). Other work could include paintings, photography, page layout designs, computer images, two-dimensional design, sculptures, models, fine crafts, mechanical drawings, and marker renderings.

For more information: artdesign.rit.edu/prospective-students/portfolio-guide

Scholarships Offered

Multiple merit-based scholarships available.

Summer Programs, Co-ops, Internships

Co-ops, internships, assistantships available. Last year, more than 4,500 students participated in co-op and internship positions with more than 3,400 hiring organizations, from large Fortune 500 companies and industry leaders, to small start-ups and world-class not-for-profits.

Special Opportunities, Facilities/Equipment

Several studios and labs available, such as our Fab Lab, equipped with 12 3D printers in addition to laser cutters, CNC routing devices, and other technology, all for you to utilize while you complete projects and class assignments.

Notable Alumni

Eric Avar, Seth Eshelman, Gary Mack, Brian Matt, Patricia Moore, Chris Petescia, Roger Remington, and Scott Wilson

CONNECTICUT

MAINE

MASSACHUSETTS

NEW HAMPSHIRE

NEW JERSEY

NEW YORK

PENNSYLVANIA

RHODE ISLAND

VERMONT

ME
VT
NY
NH
MA
PA
RI
CT
NJ

SYRACUSE UNIVERSITY

Address: 202 Crouse College, Syracuse, NY 13244
Website: *https://vpa.syr.edu/academics/design/programs/industrial-interaction-design-bid/*
Contact: *https://www.syracuse.edu/admissions/undergraduate/contact/*
Phone: (315) 443-2769
Email: admissu@syr.edu

COST OF ATTENDANCE:

Tuition & Fees: $57,591 | **Additional Expenses:** $44,448.8
Total: $80,039.80

Financial Aid: https://www.syracuse.edu/admissions/cost-and-aid/

ADDITIONAL INFORMATION:

Available Degree(s)

- Bachelor of Industrial Design (BID)

Portfolio Requirement

All first-year applicants must submit a portfolio in SlideRoom for the BID program – traditional or alternative. The portfolio should represent your breadth of your interests, ideas, skills, and willingness to experiment. Select works that represent graphic and material design and may include projects completed as assignments, in studios, or your personal exploration. Describe your pieces with a clear approach to your conceptual thinking. You will also submit a statement of interest, expanded identification of one piece in your portfolio, and a 500-word writing sample. Answering "What is design? What can it do in the world? What about design inspires you?"

Scholarships Offered

Syracuse University offers various merit-based and need-based scholarships and grants. The 1870 Scholarship covers full tuition for the full length of the undergraduate program. Artistic Scholarships are awarded to students based on talent and a maintained cumulative GPA of 2.75+.

Summer Programs, Co-ops, Internships

In the fourth year, students are encouraged to apply for study abroad programs in London or Florence. Students gain entrepreneurial skills and partner with other majors to pitch and launch their own seed-funded startup companies. By the end of the program, students will have developed an independent thesis project and exhibition that addresses contemporary global issues.

Special Opportunities, Facilities/Equipment

Studio coursework at Syracuse's BID program allows students to explore diverse areas of practice within the industrial design field today. Students engage in project-based learning, and utilize industry-standard tools and methods.

Notable Alumni

Leigh Cohen, Jon Polhamus, Drew Stanley, and Jimmy Wong

CONNECTICUT

MAINE

MASSACHUSETTS

NEW HAMPSHIRE

NEW JERSEY

NEW YORK

PENNSYLVANIA

RHODE ISLAND

VERMONT

NORTHEAST

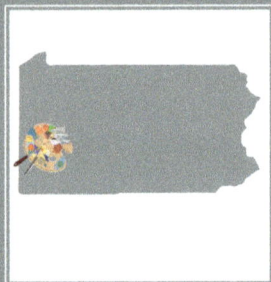

CONNECTICUT

MAINE

MASSACHUSETTS

NEW HAMPSHIRE

NEW JERSEY

NEW YORK

PENNSYLVANIA

RHODE ISLAND

VERMONT

CARNEGIE MELLON UNIVERSITY

Address: Carnegie Mellon University
Margaret Morrison Carnegie Hall, Room 110
5000 Forbes Avenue, Pittsburgh, PA 15213
Website: *https://design.cmu.edu/tags/industrial-design*
Contact: *https://design.cmu.edu/people*
Phone: (412) 268-2828
Email: info@design.cmu.edu

COST OF ATTENDANCE:

Tuition & Fees: $60,634 | **Additional Expenses:** $19,906
Total: $80,540

Financial Aid: https://www.cmu.edu/sfs/financial-aid/index.html

ADDITIONAL INFORMATION:

Available Degree(s)

- BDes (Bachelor of Design) – Products
- BDes (Bachelor of Design) – Environments
- MDes (Master of Design)
- MA in Design

Portfolio Requirements

Students must submit a video of 90 seconds or less uploaded to SlideRoom. A portfolio of no more than 18 slides from 2-D, 3-D, and 4-D work showing your creative process. You must also submit an essay on something in your neighborhood you would want to change. All materials are submitted online. "In-person interviews are not an option."

Scholarships Offered

Numerous scholarships and endowments available.

Summer Programs, Co-ops, Internships

The School of Design is a member of Design for Social Innovation and Sustainability (DESIS), an international network of design schools working in the area of social innovation research. Internships available for graduate students.

Special Opportunities, Facilities/Equipment

School of Design students have access to the university's top-flight computer science and business faculties, giving graduating designers a solid grounding in technology – hardware, software, interaction and systems – and the business acumen to succeed in the real world. Our facilities include prototyping shops, a letterpress lab, photo studios, and sophisticated computer labs. CMU offers Integrative Design, Arts, and Technology (IDeATe), allowing students to concentrate focus on cross-campus industry themes like game design, animation, and special effects, innovation and entrepreneurship, intelligent environments, and learning media design.

Notable Alumni

Fred Bould and Carroll Gantz

DREXEL UNIVERSITY

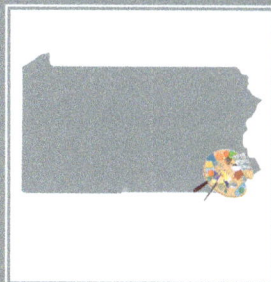

Address: URBN Center, 270B
Drexel University
3141 Chestnut Street
Philadelphia, PA 19104
Website: *https://drexel.edu/westphal/academics/undergraduate/PROD/*
Contact: *https://drexel.edu/westphal/about/contact/*
Phone: (215) 895-4421
Email: raja.schaar@drexel.edu

COST OF ATTENDANCE:

Tuition & Fees: $38,390 | **Additional Expenses:** $16,186
Total: $51,151

Financial Aid: https://drexel.edu/drexelcentral/finaid/overview/

ADDITIONAL INFORMATION:

Available Degree(s)

- BS Product Design
- MS Interior Architecture & Design

Scholarships Offered

Specific interest scholarships available, in addition to many school and private options.

Summer Programs, Co-ops, Internships

Summer program offered in industrial design. The BS Product Design program at the Westphal College is enhanced by Drexel's cooperative education experience (co-op). Product Design majors spend six months during their junior year in a full-time job in the industry, earning invaluable professional experience prior to graduation.

Special Opportunities, Facilities/Equipment

Drexel's Bachelor of Science in Product Design is housed in the URBN Center, the creative hub for Westphal College of Media Arts & Design. Product Design majors have access to labs, shops, and cutting-edge equipment with which to prototype and execute their projects. A dynamic space built for transdisciplinary collaboration, URBN is home to the Hybrid Making Lab.

This College-wide, multi-disciplinary resource is equipped with 3D printers, universal laser cutters, and large- and small-scale fabrication tools. Westphal College also manages a woodshop, printmaking studio, numerous digital media and computer labs, and individual studio workspace for Product Design students.

Notable Alumni

Juan M. Arellano, Susan Daroff, Douglas Ellington, Vicki L. Jones, William Sidney Pullman, and Rudolph Weaver

CONNECTICUT

MAINE

MASSACHUSETTS

NEW HAMPSHIRE

NEW JERSEY

NEW YORK

PENNSYLVANIA

RHODE ISLAND

VERMONT

NORTHEAST

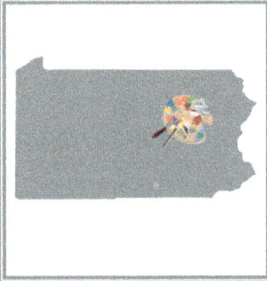

CONNECTICUT

MAINE

MASSACHUSETTS

NEW HAMPSHIRE

NEW JERSEY

NEW YORK

PENNSYLVANIA

RHODE ISLAND

VERMONT

PENNSYLVANIA COLLEGE OF TECHNOLOGY

Address: Pennsylvania College of Technology
School of Engineering Technologies, LEC, Rm. B1134
One College Avenue, Williamsport, PA 17701
Website: *https://www.pct.edu/academics/et/engineering-industrial-design-technology/industrial-design*
Contact: *https://www.pct.edu/academics/et/faculty-staff*
Phone: (570) 327-4520
Email: Contact: et@pct.edu

COST OF ATTENDANCE:

Tuition & Fees: $25,170 | **Additional Expenses:** $15,360
Total: $40,530

Financial Aid: https://www.pct.edu/admissions/financial-aid

ADDITIONAL INFORMATION:

Available Degree(s)

- BS Industrial Design
- BS Engineering Design Technology
- BS Plastics & Polymer Engineering Technology
- BS Welding & Fabrication Engineering Technology
- AA Engineering CAD Technology
- AAS Metal Fabrication Technology
- Nanofabrication Technology – Competency Credential

Scholarships Offered

Over 350 institutional, external, and program specific scholarships available.

Summer Programs, Co-ops, Internships

Paid and unpaid internships available, as well as pre-college programs and camps. Penn College summer programs have included: Spain (2022): European Sustainable Building, Historical Architecture and Art; Global Cities (2022): International Automotive Studies; Europe & the U.K.: Architecture & Sustainable Design

Special Opportunities, Facilities/Equipment

In the Industrial Design program, you'll explore functionality, ergonomics, and aesthetics. Learn how to express concepts using rendering software. The Industrial Design Studio comes complete with a model shop and work benches. Fun organizations like SIMS and SWORD, and study abroad opportunities available.

Notable Alumni

Tom Ask, Jeffrey Freeman, Cory Karges, and Richard Wood

RHODE ISLAND SCHOOL OF DESIGN

Address: Rhode Island School of Design
Two College Street
Providence, RI 02903-2784
Website: *https://www.risd.edu/academics/industrial-design*
Contact: *https://www.risd.edu/academics/industrial-design/contact*
Phone: (401) 454-6160
Email: mbuttenh@risd.edu

COST OF ATTENDANCE:

Tuition & Fees: $57,505 | **Additional Expenses:** $21,436
Total: $78,941

Financial Aid: https://www.risd.edu/student-financial-services

ADDITIONAL INFORMATION:

Available Degree(s)

- BFA Industrial Design
- MID (Master of Industrial Design)

Portfolio Required

After completing the Common Application, students will submit a SlideRoom supplement, presenting 12-20 of their recent work. RISD requests finished pieces, drawings from direct observation, and no more than three pieces that show research and prep work. RISD's admissions are competitive so curate and edit the pieces you choose to submit.

Scholarships Offered

Multiple school, private, and special scholarships available.

Summer Programs, Co-ops, Internships

Pre-college program and summer camps, co-ops and internships are available.

Special Opportunities, Facilities/Equipment

Cross-registration program with Brown University. Facilities include the woodshop, model shop, metal/machine shop, fabrication technology, and software.

Notable Alumni

Fredrick Warren Allen, Janine Antoni, Tanya Aguiniga, Ross Palmer Beecher, Howard Ben Tre, John Benson, Huma Bhabha, Martin Blank, Dale Chihuly, Alison Croney, Shepard Fairey, Katherine Gray, Lauren Goodman, Paul Housberg, Karen LaMonte, Casper Nagel, Mary Shaffer, Therman Statom, Wing Yau, and Toots Zynsky

CONNECTICUT

MAINE

MASSACHUSETTS

NEW HAMPSHIRE

NEW JERSEY

NEW YORK

PENNSYLVANIA

RHODE ISLAND

VERMONT

NORTHEAST

CHAPTER 14
REGION TWO

MIDWEST

ILLINOIS

INDIANA

IOWA

KANSAS

MICHIGAN

MINNESOTA

MISSOURI

NEBRASKA

NORTH DAKOTA

OHIO

SOUTH DAKOTA

WISCONSIN

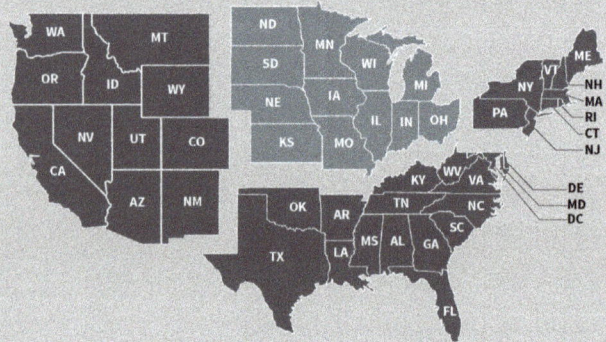

11 *Programs* | 12 *States*

1. *IL - University of Illinois, Chicago*
2. *IL - University of Illinois, Urbana-Champaign*
3. *IN - Purdue University*
4. *IN - University of Notre Dame*
5. *IA - Iowa State University*
6. *MI - Lawrence Technological University*
7. *MN - University of Minnesota, Twin Cities*
8. *OH - Cedarville University*
9. *OH - The Ohio State University*
10. *OH - University of Cincinnati*
11. *WI - University of Wisconsin, Stout*

INDUSTRIAL DESIGN PROGRAMS

School	Avg. GPA, SAT Evidence-Based Reading Writing (ERW), SAT Math (M), and ACT Composite (C) Early Decision (ED): Yes/No	Admission Statistics	Program(s)
University of Illinois, Chicago 1200 W Harrison St, Chicago, IL 60607	GPA: N/A SAT (ERW): 510-610 SAT (M): 520-640 ACT (C): 21-29 ED: No	Overall College Admit Rate: 73% Undergrad Enrollment: 21,921 Total Enrollment: 33,518	BA Industrial Design Bachelor of Design, Industrial Design MDes Master of Design in Industrial Design
University of Illinois Urbana-Champaign (UIUC) 901 West Illinois Street, Urbana, IL 61801	GPA: N/A SAT (ERW): 590-700 SAT (M): 620-770 ACT (C): 27-33 ED: Yes	Overall College Admit Rate: 50% Undergrad Enrollment: 34,559 Total Enrollment: 56,257	BFA Industrial Design MFA Industrial Design
Purdue University Purdue University, West Lafayette, IN 47907	GPA: 3.67 SAT (ERW): 590-690 SAT (M): 600-740 ACT (C): 25-33 ED: No	Overall College Admit Rate: 67% Undergrad Enrollment: 34,920 Total Enrollment: 45,869	BFA Industrial Design MFA Industrial Design
University of Notre Dame University of Notre Dame, Notre Dame, IN 46556	GPA: N/A SAT (ERW): 690-760 SAT (M): 710-790 ACT (C): 32-35 ED: Yes	Overall College Admit Rate: 19% Undergrad Enrollment: 8,874 Total Enrollment: 12,809	BA Industrial Design BFA Industrial Design MFA Industrial Design
Iowa State University 715 Bissell Rd, Ames, IA 50011	GPA: 3.71 SAT (ERW): 480-630 SAT (M): 530-680 ACT (C): 21-28 ED: No	Overall College Admit Rate: 88% Undergrad Enrollment: 26,843 Total Enrollment: 31,822	BS Industrial Design Master of Science in Industrial Design

School	Avg. GPA, SAT Evidence-Based Reading Writing (ERW), SAT Math (M), and ACT Composite (C) Early Decision (ED): Yes/No	Admission Statistics	Program(s)
Lawrence Technological University 21000 West Ten Mile Road, Southfield, MI 48075	GPA: 3.5 SAT (ERW): 500-620 SAT (M): 520-660 ACT (C): 21-29 ED: No	Admit Rate: 82% Undergrad Enrollment: 2,138 Total Enrollment: 2,812	BS Industrial Design BS Transportation Design
University of Minnesota, Twin Cities 330 21st Ave S., Minneapolis, MN 55455	GPA: N/A SAT (ERW): 600-700 SAT (M): 640-760 ACT (C): 25-31 ED: No	Overall College Admit Rate: 70% Undergrad Enrollment: 36,061 Total Enrollment: 52,017	BS Product Design MS Product Design
Cedarville University 251 N. Main St., Cedarville, OH 45314	GPA: 3.91 SAT (ERW): 570-680 SAT (M): 540-670 ACT (C): 23-30 ED: No	Overall College Admit Rate: 59% Undergrad Enrollment: 4,024 Total Enrollment: 4,461	BS Industrial & Innovative Design
Ohio State University 1849 Cannon Drive, Columbus, OH 43210	GPA: N/A SAT (ERW): 590-690 SAT (M): 620-740 ACT (C): 26-32 ED: No	Overall College Admit Rate: 87% Undergrad Enrollment: 19,284 Total Enrollment: 25,714	Bachelor of Science in Design, Industrial Design MFA Design Research and Development

MIDWEST

INDUSTRIAL DESIGN PROGRAMS

School	Avg. GPA, SAT Evidence-Based Reading Writing (ERW), SAT Math (M), and ACT Composite (C) Early Decision (ED): Yes/No	Admission Statistics	Program(s)
University of Cincinnati 2600 Clifton Ave, Cincinnati, OH 45221	GPA: 3.7 SAT (ERW): 560-650 SAT (M): 560-680 ACT (C): 23-29 ED: No	Overall College Admit Rate: 76% Undergrad Enrollment: 29,933 Total Enrollment: 40,826	BS Industrial Design Masters in Design
University of Wisconsin, Stout 712 Broadway St S, Menomonie, WI 54751	GPA: N/A SAT (ERW): N/A SAT (M): N/A ACT (C): 20-25 ED: No	Overall College Admit Rate: 90% Undergrad Enrollment: 6,889 Total Enrollment: 7,970	BFA Industrial Design MFA in Design

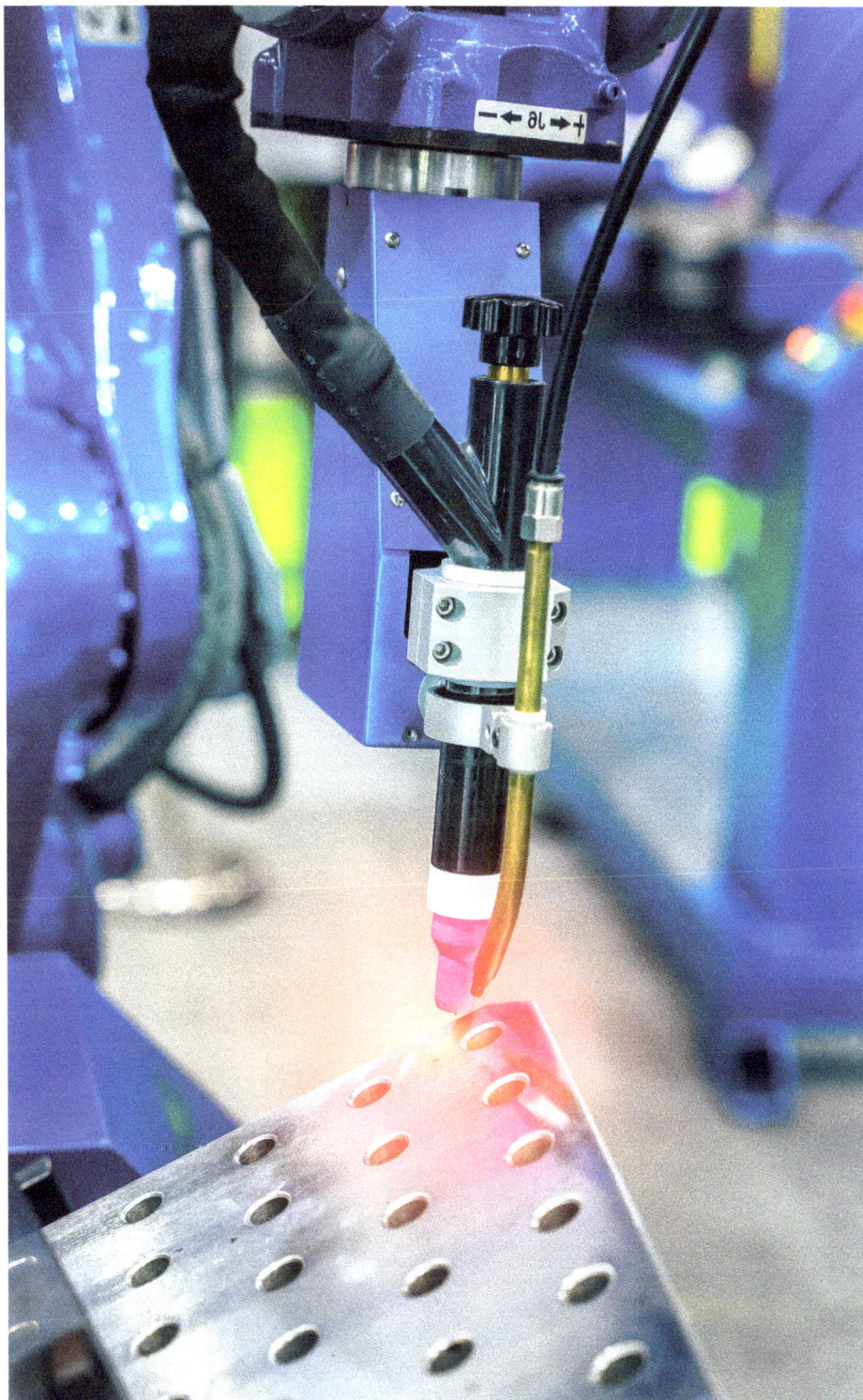

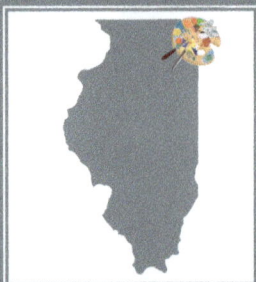

ILLINOIS

INDIANA

IOWA

KANSAS

MICHIGAN

MINNESOTA

MISSOURI

NEBRASKA

NORTH DAKOTA

OHIO

SOUTH DAKOTA

WISCONSIN

UNIVERSITY OF ILLINOIS – CHICAGO

Address: The University of Illinois – Chicago
School of Design (MC 036)
845 West Harrison Street
Chicago, IL 60607-7038
Website: *www.design.uic.edu*
Contact: *https://design.uic.edu/node/49*
Phone: (312) 996-2611
Email: design@uic.edu

COST OF ATTENDANCE:

Tuition & Fees: $26,986 | **Additional Expenses:** $15,832
Total: $42,818

Financial Aid: https://financialaid.uic.edu/

ADDITIONAL INFORMATION:

Available Degree(s)

- BA Industrial Design
- BDes Bachelor of Design – Industrial Design
- MDes Master of Design in Industrial Design

Scholarships Offered

Various scholarship opportunities.

Summer Programs, Co-ops, Internships

Internships are encouraged and the list of companies where UIC students/graduates work is impressive.

Special Opportunities, Facilities/Equipment

State of the art facilities, including The UIC Design Print Lab offering the latest in digital imaging services including color laser, large format, and risograph printing, the Project Lab, Fabrication Lab, and the Electronic Visualization Lab.

Notable Alumni

Michael G. Turnbull

UNIVERSITY OF ILLINOIS – URBANA-CHAMPAIGN

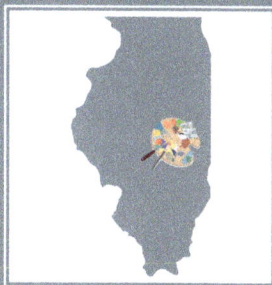

Address: University of Illinois, Urbana-Champaign
143 Art and Design Building
408 E. Peabody Drive
Champaign, IL 61820
Website: *https://art.illinois.edu/*
Contact: *https://art.illinois.edu/about/contact-us/*
Phone: (217) 333-6632
Email: mavery@illinois.edu

COST OF ATTENDANCE:

Tuition & Fees: $22,324 | **Additional Expenses:** $16,420
Total: $38,744

Financial Aid: https://admissions.illinois.edu/Invest/financial-aid

ADDITIONAL INFORMATION:

Available Degree(s)

- BFA Industrial Design
- MFA Industrial Design

Scholarships Offered

Several school merit and private scholarships available.

Summer Programs, Co-ops, Internships

Annual fairs are hosted by the College of Fine and Applied Arts to pair School of Art & Design students with on-campus and off-campus jobs and for-credit internships. Corporate and faculty collabs.

Special Opportunities, Facilities/Equipment

Facilities include 3D fabrication labs, ceramics, lab, darkroon, digital labs, and textile lab. Students work with 2-D, 3-D, CAD, computer modeling, rapid prototyping, and animation programs, engineering, and woodshop. Additional labs available in metals, ceramics, graphic design, and photography.

Krannert Art Museum – 8,000+ pieces
Ricker Library of Architecture and Art

Notable Alumni

Bill Stumpf and Craig Vetter

ILLINOIS

INDIANA

IOWA

KANSAS

MICHIGAN

MINNESOTA

MISSOURI

NEBRASKA

NORTH DAKOTA

OHIO

SOUTH DAKOTA

WISCONSIN

MIDWEST

PURDUE UNIVERSITY – WEST LAFAYETTE

Address: Pao Hall of Visual and Performing Arts
Purdue University
552 W. Wood Street
West Lafayette, IN 47907
Website: *https://www.cla.purdue.edu/academic/rueffschool/ad/industrial/Undegrad_Program.html*
Contact: *https://www.cla.purdue.edu/about/contact.html*
Phone: (765) 494-8662
Email: ADinfo@purdue.edu

COST OF ATTENDANCE:

Tuition & Fees: $28,794 | **Additional Expenses:** $12,820
Total: $41,614

Financial Aid: https://www.purdue.edu/dfa/

ADDITIONAL INFORMATION:

Available Degree(s)

- BFA Industrial Design
- MFA Industrial Design

Scholarships Offered

Many need-based, merit and college-wide scholarships available.

Summer Programs, Co-ops, Internships

ID students gain experience through internships and co-ops in manufacturing and product design for top companies and consultancies. During junior and senior years, student projects include working directly with professionals on their projects.

Special Opportunities, Facilities/Equipment

Students create designs using traditional wood and metal shop equipment, alongside digital tools - laser cutter, a CNC machine, and 3-D printers. After sophomore review, ID students have dedicated design studios, fully computerized and available with 24-hour access. Advanced students have access to CNC rapid prototyping. Students learn software including Rhino 3D, Solidworks, and Keyshot for computer modeling and rendering. Students use Adobe Photoshop and InDesign for presentations and rendering and Adobe DreamWeaver, AfterEffects, Axure RP, Sketch, Atlas. TI for interaction design and user experience analysis.

Notable Alumni

Orville Redenbacher, Venu Srinivasan, and Lebbeus Woods

UNIVERSITY OF NOTRE DAME

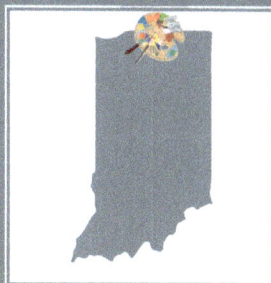

Address: University of Notre Dame
306 Riley Hall of Art & Design
Notre Dame, IN 46556
Website: *https://artdept.nd.edu/undergraduate-program/design/industrial-design/*
Contact: *https://artdept.nd.edu/faculty/contact/*
Phone: (574) 631-7602
Email: art.1@nd.edu

COST OF ATTENDANCE:

Tuition & Fees: $60,010 | **Additional Expenses:** $18,580
Total: $78,590

Financial Aid: https://financialaid.nd.edu/

ADDITIONAL INFORMATION:

Available Degree(s)

- BA Industrial Design
- BFA Industrial Design
- MFA Industrial Design

Scholarships Offered

Many available through school and College of Arts and Letters.

Summer Programs, Co-ops, Internships

Summer internships are encouraged. The Industrial Design program maintains relationships with design firms in the Chicago area and across the country from alumni contacts. Internships may also substitute for degree credit.

Special Opportunities, Facilities/Equipment

Ceramics studio, creative computing group, digital print studio, digital fabrication lab, metal shop and foundry, photo studios, woodshop, 2D Computer Lab, 3D Computer Lab, and West Lake Design Studio.

BFA Thesis Exhibition, Max & Emma Lecture Series, and second majors

Notable Alumni

Sophia Bevacqua, Emily Hoffman, Alex Lobos, Will McLeod, Mallory McMorrow, Eileen Murphy, Mansour Ourasanah, Justin Schneider, Jonathan Sundy, and Jackson Wrede

ILLINOIS

INDIANA

IOWA

KANSAS

MICHIGAN

MINNESOTA

MISSOURI

NEBRASKA

NORTH DAKOTA

OHIO

SOUTH DAKOTA

WISCONSIN

MIDWEST

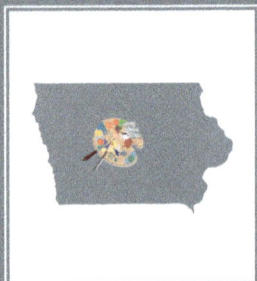

ILLINOIS

INDIANA

IOWA

KANSAS

MICHIGAN

MINNESOTA

MISSOURI

NEBRASKA

NORTH DAKOTA

OHIO

SOUTH DAKOTA

WISCONSIN

IOWA STATE UNIVERSITY

Address: Iowa State University
290 Design, 715 Bissell Road
Ames, IA 50011-1066
Website: *https://www.design.iastate.edu/industrial-design/*
Contact: *https://www.design.iastate.edu/industrial-design/contact/*
Phone: (515) 294-0816
Email: brycebonn@iastate.edu

COST OF ATTENDANCE:

Tuition & Fees: $25,446 | **Additional Expenses:** $12,518
Total: $37,964

Financial Aid: https://www.financialaid.iastate.edu/

ADDITIONAL INFORMATION:

Available Degree(s)

- BS Industrial Design
- MSID (Master of Science in Industrial Design)

Scholarships Offered

Numerous institutional and private scholarships available.

Summer Programs, Co-ops, Internships

The College of Design hosts one career fair dedicated to design and also participates in the Big 12 Virtual Career Fair. Students have access to CyHire for job and internship seeking, GoinGlobal for international job seeking, and Big Interview.

Studio credits taken in study abroad industrial design programs count as part of the 12 required Experiential Learning credits.

Special Opportunities, Facilities/Equipment

Industrial Design's fabrication workshop is equivalent or above industry standards - CNC routers, plastic and ceramic injection molds, vacuum former, 3D printer, laser cutter, a traditional woodshop, and virtual reality systems.

Design Career Services offers individual appointments, presentations, mock interviews, resume reviews, and more. Students focus on portfolio development and professional practice.

NSF Pilot Study, I-FIT Competitions, STEM Outreach, Senior Show, juried exhibits, innovation pitch contests, creativity contests, and CYstarters Demo Day.

Notable Alumni

Oshoke Pamela Abalu, Jeremy Caniglia, Michael Mabry, Conde McCullough, and Richard Schultz.

LAWRENCE TECHNOLOGICAL UNIVERSITY

Address: College of Art & Design
Lawrence Technological University
21000 West Ten Mile Road
Southfield, MI 48075-1058
Website: *https://www.ltu.edu/architecture_and_design/art_design/bs_industrial_design.asp*
Contact: *https://www.ltu.edu/contacts/*
Phone: (248) 204-2835
Email: admissions@ltu.edu

COST OF ATTENDANCE:

Tuition & Fees: $37,680 | **Additional Expenses:** $1,968
Total: $39,648

Financial Aid: https://www.ltu.edu/financial_aid/

ADDITIONAL INFORMATION:

Available Degree(s)

- BS Industrial Design
- BS Transportation Design

Scholarships Offered

Institutional and private scholarships available for both general and program specific preferences.

Summer Programs, Co-ops, Internships

Summer Critical Practice Programs

Special Opportunities, Facilities/Equipment

The Industrial Design program is designed to facilitate cross-disciplinary projects, collaborate with industry professionals, and design and develop product concepts throughout the 4-year core curriculum. Facilities include dedicated studio space and cutting-edge printing and fabrication labs.

The project-centered curriculum focuses on sustainability, ergonomics, user experience, product psychology, business case assessment, entrepreneurship, leadership, packaging, and cultural geography.

Students in Transportation Design pursue Aviation Design, Automotive Design, Automotive Specialty Equipment Design, Bike Design, Yacht & Boat Design, Motorcycle Design, Mass Transit Design, Mobility Design.

Notable Alumni

Mark Farlow and Paul Urbanek

ILLINOIS

INDIANA

IOWA

KANSAS

MICHIGAN

MINNESOTA

MISSOURI

NEBRASKA

NORTH DAKOTA

OHIO

SOUTH DAKOTA

WISCONSIN

MIDWEST

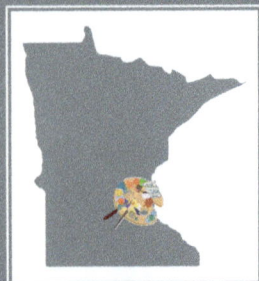

ILLINOIS

INDIANA

IOWA

KANSAS

MICHIGAN

MINNESOTA

MISSOURI

NEBRASKA

NORTH DAKOTA

OHIO

SOUTH DAKOTA

WISCONSIN

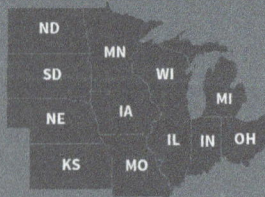

UNIVERSITY OF MINNESOTA, TWIN CITIES

Address: 330 21st Ave S., Minneapolis, MN 55455
Website: *https://design.umn.edu/academics/programs/about-product-design*
Contact: *https://design.umn.edu/node/53191*
Phone: (612) 625-6860
Email: pdesk@umn.edu

COST OF ATTENDANCE:

Tuition & Fees: $34,556 | **Additional Expenses:** $15,580
Total: $51,036

Financial Aid: https://admissions.tc.umn.edu/cost-aid/financial-aid

ADDITIONAL INFORMATION:

Available Degree(s)

- BS Product Design
- MS Product Design

Scholarships Offered

College of Design students can apply for College-specific scholarships as well as University-wide scholarships.

Summer Programs, Co-ops, Internships

At least one internship is required. Students develop ongoing mentoring relationships with alumni and industry professionals both inside and outside the classroom.

Product design students can gain valuable cultural experiences while earning credits in places like London, Copenhagen, and Aukland.

Special Opportunities, Facilities/Equipment

Human Dimensioning Lab, Wearable Tech Lab, Digital Design Center, Imaging lab, state of the art equipment. Study Abroad program.

Students must pass the portfolio review to continue.

Notable Alumni

Richard Gurley Drew, Arthur Fry, and Reynold B. Johnson

CEDARVILLE UNIVERSITY

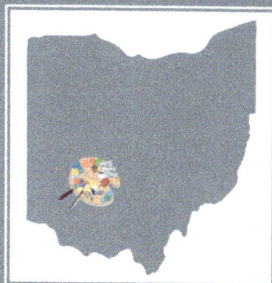

Address: Cedarville University
Department of Art, Design, and Theatre
251 N. Main St., Cedarville, OH 45314
Website: *https://www.cedarville.edu/academic-schools-and-departments/art-design-theatre*
Contact: *https://www.cedarville.edu/academic-schools-and-departments/art-design-theatre/contact-us*
Phone: (937) 766-3437
Email: https://www.cedarville.edu/why-cedarville/contact-form?epart1=carloschang&toname=Carlos+Chang

COST OF ATTENDANCE:

Tuition & Fees: $37,896 | **Additional Expenses:** $12,494
Total: $50,390

Financial Aid: https://www.cedarville.edu/offices/financial-aid/undergraduate

ADDITIONAL INFORMATION:

Available Degree(s)

- BS Industrial & Innovative Design

Scholarships Offered

In 2022, 100% of new freshmen received scholarships. Average Award: $20,150. Academic scholarships are renewable for four years if they meet academic standards.

Summer Programs, Co-ops, Internships

Internships available.

Special Opportunities, Facilities/Equipment

Cedarville partners with the International Center for Creativity (ICC) in their recently renovated facilities in Dublin, Ohio, near Columbus. Students complete two years on the Cedarville campus completing the Bible minor and general ed courses.

Junior and senior years are spent at ICC's unique and picturesque professional design studios. Students are taught skills needed for 3D design - design thinking, consumer insights research, rapid sketch ideation, prototyping, 3D CAD modeling, marketing-based product launches, and presentations. Students pursue consumer product design, exterior architectural design, interior architectural design, and transportation design.

Notable Alumni

Jenna Ellis, Valde Garcia, and Mark Keough

ILLINOIS

INDIANA

IOWA

KANSAS

MICHIGAN

MINNESOTA

MISSOURI

NEBRASKA

NORTH DAKOTA

OHIO

SOUTH DAKOTA

WISCONSIN

MIDWEST

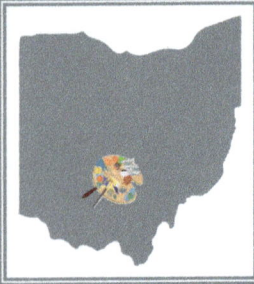

ILLINOIS

INDIANA

IOWA

KANSAS

MICHIGAN

MINNESOTA

MISSOURI

NEBRASKA

NORTH DAKOTA

OHIO

SOUTH DAKOTA

WISCONSIN

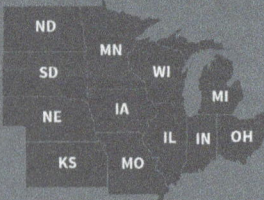

OHIO STATE UNIVERSITY

Address: Ohio State University
Department of Design
100 Hayes Hall, 108 Oval Mall
Columbus, OH 43210
Website: *https://design.osu.edu/undergrad/programs/ind*
Contact: *https://design.osu.edu/contact*
Phone: (614) 292-6746
Email: design@osu.edu

COST OF ATTENDANCE:

Tuition & Fees: $35,019 | **Additional Expenses:** $13,352
Total: $48,371

Financial Aid: http://undergrad.osu.edu/cost-and-aid/financial-aid

ADDITIONAL INFORMATION:

Available Degree(s)

- BSD Industrial Design
- MFA Design Research and Development

Scholarships Offered

Six scholarships offered by the Department of Design.

Summer Programs, Co-ops, Internships

Co-op and internship opportunities through Handshake, as well as co-ops and externships.

Special Opportunities, Facilities/Equipment

Facilities include studios, ACCAD, and the DESIS Lab. Students have career fairs, projects, and exhibitions to further enhance their learning experience. Students must have a laptop and may use in the course of their study Adobe Creative Cloud, SolidWorks, and KeyShot.

Students begin in the Design Foundations sequence and must prepare a portfolio during the first year and be accepted to continue as a Design Foundations student.

Notable Alumni

Cynthia E. Smith and Luisa V. Talamas

UNIVERSITY OF CINCINNATI

Address: University of Cincinnati
Student Affairs
College of Design, Architecture, and Planning (DAAP)
School of Design, P.O. Box 210016
Cincinnati, OH 45221-0016
Website: *https://daap.uc.edu/academic-programs/school-of-design/industrial-design.html*
Contact:
Phone: (513) 556-1376
Email: daap-admissions@uc.edu

COST OF ATTENDANCE:

Tuition & Fees: $29,183 | **Additional Expenses:** $15,652
Total: $44,835

Financial Aid: https://financialaid.uc.edu/

ADDITIONAL INFORMATION:

Available Degree(s)

- BS Industrial Design
- MDes (Masters in Design)

Scholarships Offered

Numerous school and dept. scholarships available, including research and study abroad.

Summer Programs, Co-ops, Internships

DAAPcamps. Co-ops begin sophmore year.

Special Opportunities, Facilities/Equipment

The college supports a Rapid Prototyping Center, which is the home of state-of-the-art equipment that allows students to use CAD (computer-aided design) models, create physical models using three basic methods: 3-D printing, large format laser-cutting, and CNC (computer numeric control) devices, including a Komo CNC Router. Educational opportunities include organized travel semesters, foreign study semesters and student exchange programs in England, Germany and Denmark. Third-year students can focus on product or transportation design.

Notable Alumni

Charlie Bailey, Michael Graves, Ronald Howes, and George Speri Sperti

ILLINOIS

INDIANA

IOWA

KANSAS

MICHIGAN

MINNESOTA

MISSOURI

NEBRASKA

NORTH DAKOTA

OHIO

SOUTH DAKOTA

WISCONSIN

MIDWEST

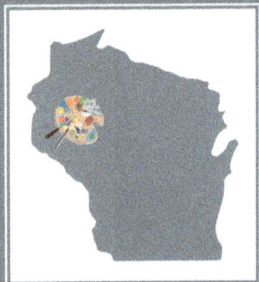

ILLINOIS

INDIANA

IOWA

KANSAS

MICHIGAN

MINNESOTA

MISSOURI

NEBRASKA

NORTH DAKOTA

OHIO

SOUTH DAKOTA

WISCONSIN

UNIVERSITY OF WISCONSIN, STOUT

Address: University of Wisconsin, Stout
College of Arts, Communication, Humanities and Social Sciences
Design Department, School of Art & Design
712 South Broadway Street
Menomonie, WI 54751
Website: *https://www.uwstout.edu/programs/bfa-industrial-design*
Contact: *https://www.uwstout.edu/directory/astwoodj*
Phone: (715) 232-3699
Email: astwoodj@uwstout.edu

COST OF ATTENDANCE:

In-State Tuition & Fees: $9,552 | **Additional Expenses:** $11,022
Total: $20,574

Out-of-State Tuition & Fees: $17,819 | **Additional Expenses:** $11,022
Total: $28,841

Financial Aid: https://www.uwstout.edu/admissions-aid/paying-college/financial-aid

ADDITIONAL INFORMATION:

Available Degree(s)

- BFA Industrial Design
- MFA in Design

Scholarships Offered

In addition to the NEW Blue Devil First-Year Student Scholarship offered to all students meeting the criteria, there are also design-specific scholarships are offered. Additionally, Stout Scholars receive $5,000 and there is a scholarship for students who are out-of-state. The Honors College Scholarship is an additional $1,000. Transfer students are eligible for a scholarship if they have a 3.0 and are transferring between 24 – 90 credits.

Summer Programs, Co-ops, Internships

The ID studio consists of several spaces: a comfortable workspace for instruction and creation and where industry leaders conduct workshops, a modeling room with 3D printers, a spray booth, and storage and display spaces.

ID students learn to design, manufacture, and package the products we use every day - sports cars, shoes, wearable devices, furniture, and cellphones.

Special Opportunities, Facilities/Equipment

Study abroad program. The ID studio consists of several spaces: a comfortable workspace for instruction and creation and where professional speakers hold workshops, room 216A where all Industrial Design students work on their modeling, room 216B which houses 3D printers, a spray booth, and storage and display spaces.

Notable Alumni

Reed Crawford

CHAPTER 15

REGION THREE

SOUTH

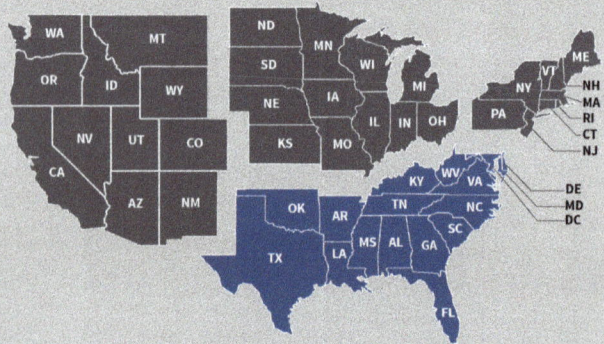

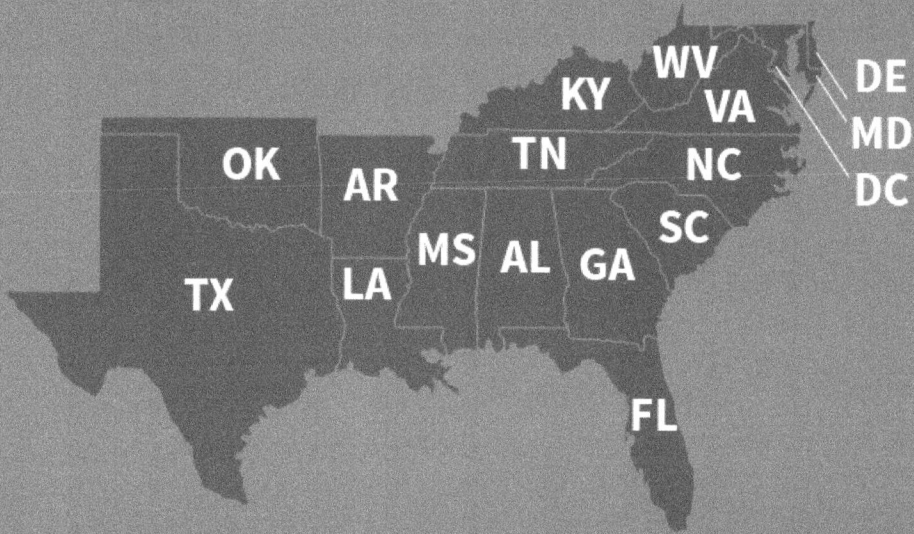

8 Programs | 16 States

1. AL - Auburn University
2. GA - Georgia Institute of Technology
3. GA - Savannah College of Art & Design
4. LA - University of Louisiana, Lafayette

5. NC - Appalachian State University
6. NC - North Carolina State University
7. TX - University of Houston
8. VA - Virginia Tech

INDUSTRIAL DESIGN PROGRAMS

School	Avg. GPA, SAT Evidence-Based Reading Writing (ERW), SAT Math (M), and ACT Composite (C) Early Decision (ED): Yes/No	Admission Statistics	Program(s)
Auburn University 210 Spidle Hall, Auburn, AL 36849	GPA: 3.97 SAT (ERW): 590-650 SAT (M): 570-670 ACT (C): 25-31 ED: No	Admit Rate: 85% Undergrad Enrollment: 24,505 Total Enrollment: 30,737	BS Environmental Design BS Industrial Design Masters in Industrial Design
Georgia Institute of Technology Georgia Institute of Technology, North Ave NW, Atlanta, GA 30332	GPA: 4.09 SAT (ERW): 670-740 SAT (M): 700-790 ACT (C): 31-35 ED: No	Overall College Admit Rate: 21% Undergrad Enrollment: 16,561 Total Enrollment: 39,771	BS Industrial Design Masters in Industrial Design
Savannah College of Art & Design (SCAD) 342 Bull St., Savannah, GA 31401	GPA: 3.6 SAT (ERW): 540-640 SAT (M): 500-600 ACT (C): 20-27 ED: No	Admit Rate: 78% Undergrad Enrollment: 11,679 Total Enrollment: 14,265	BFA Industrial Design MFA Industrial Design MA Industrial Design
University of Louisiana, Lafayette 104 E University Ave, Lafayette, LA 70504	GPA: N/A SAT (ERW): 510-620 SAT (M): 490-590 ACT (C): 20-26 ED: No	Overall College Admit Rate: 67% Undergrad Enrollment: 14,020 Total Enrollment: 16,450	BS Industrial Design
Appalachian State University 287 Rivers Street, Boone, NC 28608	GPA: 3.98 SAT (ERW): 540-630 SAT (M): 530-610 ACT (C): 22-27 ED: No	Overall College Admit Rate: 80% Undergrad Enrollment: 18,061 Total Enrollment: 20,023	BS Product Design

School	Avg. GPA, SAT Evidence-Based Reading Writing (ERW), SAT Math (M), and ACT Composite (C) Early Decision (ED): Yes/No	Admission Statistics	Program(s)
North Carolina State University (NC State) 50 Pullen Road, Raleigh, NC 27695	GPA: 3.8 SAT (ERW): 620-690 SAT (M): 630-730 ACT (C): 27-32 ED: No	Overall College Admit Rate: 46% Undergrad Enrollment: 26,150 Total Enrollment: 36,042	Bachelor of Industrial Design Masters in Industrial Design
University of Houston 4200 Elgin Street, Room 122, Houston, TX 77204	GPA: 3.73 SAT (ERW): 560-650 SAT (M): 560-660 ACT (C): 22-28 ED: No	Overall College Admit Rate: 63% Undergrad Enrollment: 39,165 Total Enrollment: 47,090	BS Industrial Design MS Industrial Design
Virginia Polytechnic Institute and State University (Virginia Tech) 1325 Perry Street, Blacksburg, VA 24061	GPA: 3.96 SAT (ERW): 590-680 SAT (M): 580-690 ACT (C): 25-31 ED: Yes	Overall College Admit Rate: 66% Undergrad Enrollment: 30,020 Total Enrollment: 37,024	BS Industrial Design; BS Packaging Systems Design MS in Human-Centered Design

SOUTH

ALABAMA

ARKANSAS

DELAWARE

DISTRICT OF COLUMBIA

FLORIDA

GEORGIA

KENTUCKY

LOUISIANA

MARYLAND

MISSISSIPPI

NORTH CAROLINA

OKLAHOMA

SOUTH CAROLINA

TENNESSEE

TEXAS

VIRGINIA

WEST VIRGINIA

AUBURN UNIVERSITY

Address: Auburn University
207 Wallace Hall
AL 36849
Website: *https://www.auburn.edu/ind/index.php*
Contact: *https://cadc.auburn.edu/contact/*
Phone: (334) 844-2364
Email: lundece@auburn.edu

COST OF ATTENDANCE:

Tuition & Fees: $34,146 | **Additional Expenses:** $10,912
Total: $45,058

Financial Aid: https://www.auburn.edu/administration/business-finance/finaid/

ADDITIONAL INFORMATION:

Available Degree(s)

- BS Environmental Design
- BS Industrial Design
- MID (Masters in Industrial Design)

Scholarships Offered

Over a hundred undergraduate scholarships and an assistantship program for graduate students.

Summer Programs, Co-ops, Internships

Students have the opportunity to participate in collaborative industry projects throughout school, working with clients while analyzing and producing design solutions for companies. Industry collaborations include projects with 3M, IBM, Frigidaire, NASA, Brother International, Broan-Nutone, and Emerson Tool Company.

Summer Design Studio – 10-week Industrial Design First Year Studio, required for admission in the Industrial Design Professional Program. Students with the top 45 GPAs proceed to the professional program.

Special Opportunities, Facilities/Equipment

Auburn University offers training and instruction in user research, design methodology, concept development, prototyping, and computer simulation/modeling. Annual international studio programs are provided in both Ireland and Taiwan.

Students share studios and workshops at colleges in Ireland, Northern Island, Scotland, England, Taiwan, and Hong Kong.

Notable Alumni

Jennifer Bonner, J.T. Carter, Tom Hardy, Paul Hedgepath, Samuel Mockabee, and Paul Rudolph

GEORGIA INSTITUTE OF TECHNOLOGY

Address: Georgia Institute of Technology
247 Fourth St. NW
Atlanta, GA 30332
Website: *https://id.gatech.edu/*
Contact: *https://id.gatech.edu/contact-us*
Phone: (404) 894-4874
Email: sid-questions@design.gatech.edu

COST OF ATTENDANCE:

Tuition & Fees: $33,964 | **Additional Expenses:** $16,306
Total: $50,270

Financial Aid: http://finaid.gatech.edu/

ADDITIONAL INFORMATION:

Available Degree(s)

- BS Industrial Design
- MID (Masters in Industrial Design)

Portfolio Requirement

Portfolios are not required but they are valuable to provide additional insight into your training, aspirations, and qualifications.

Scholarships Offered

The Institute awards undergraduates more than $105 million in need and merit-based aid. Additionally, many of our in-state students are eligible for the Hope and Zell Miller merit scholarships, as well as various institutional and outside scholarships.

Summer Programs, Co-ops, Internships

The Georgia Tech Undergraduate Co-op Program is a five-year, academic program with paid practical work experience directly related to the student's major. The Internship Program is an academic program designed to complement a student's formal education with practical work experience. The internships are single-semester, major related full-time or part-time work experiences that help students better understand the "real world" applications of their academic studies.

Special Opportunities, Facilities/Equipment

Study abroad. Georgia Tech has a campus in France where many students study.

Facilities include the Interactive Product Design Lab, REAR LAb, Body Scan LAb, the GH HMI Lab, prototyping machines, printing/plotting resources, 3D printing, thermoforming, laser cutting, computers, and interactive software. The Work Room, open 24/7 has belt sanders, disc sanders, drill press, foredom, milling machine, and sandpaper.

Notable Alumni

Jan Lorenc, L. W. "Chip" Robert, Jr., and Vern Yip

ALABAMA

ARKANSAS

DELAWARE

DISTRICT OF COLUMBIA

FLORIDA

GEORGIA

KENTUCKY

LOUISIANA

MARYLAND

MISSISSIPPI

NORTH CAROLINA

OKLAHOMA

SOUTH CAROLINA

TENNESSEE

TEXAS

VIRGINIA

WEST VIRGINIA

SOUTH

ALABAMA

ARKANSAS

DELAWARE

DISTRICT OF
COLUMBIA

FLORIDA

GEORGIA

KENTUCKY

LOUISIANA

MARYLAND

MISSISSIPPI

NORTH CAROLINA

OKLAHOMA

SOUTH CAROLINA

TENNESSEE

TEXAS

VIRGINIA

WEST VIRGINIA

SAVANNAH COLLEGE OF ART & DESIGN

Address: Savannah College of Art & Design
Admission Department
P.O. Box 2072
Savannah, GA 31402-2072
Website: *https://www.scad.edu/academics/programs/industrial-design*
Contact: *https://www.scad.edu/about/contact*
Phone: (800) 869-7223
Email: sod@scad.edu

COST OF ATTENDANCE:

Tuition & Fees: $39,620 | **Additional Expenses:** $19,629
Total: $59,249

Financial Aid: https://www.scad.edu/admission/financial-aid-and-scholarships

ADDITIONAL INFORMATION:

Available Degree(s)

- MFA Industrial Design
- MA Industrial Design

Scholarships Offered

80% of new applicants receive scholarships. Merit scholarships are available and do not need to be repaid. High school students grades 7-12 can compete for art and writing awards. There are also SCAD Challenge Awards. Submit pieces to SlideRoom in the categories in which you want to compete in the contest. Undergraduate challenge categories include 2D, 3D, Animation & Game Design, Fashion, Film, Graphic Design, Performing Arts, Photography, and Writing.

Summer Programs, Co-ops, Internships

Summer seminars and pre-college programs.

Special Opportunities, Facilities/Equipment

Study abroad program. Our students study in the renowned SCAD Gulfstream Center for Design, a 45,000-square-foot facility with studios and workshops with resources for wood, metal, plastics, and composites. Computer programming, mixed reality, design thinking, and STEM collide in The Shed.

Notable Alumni

Heather Doram and Jefferson Wood

UNIVERSITY OF LOUISIANA, LAFAYETTE

Address: University of Louisiana, Lafayette
School of Architecture and Design
421 East Lewis Street
Lafayette, LA 70503
Website: *https://architecture.louisiana.edu/programs/industrial-design*
Contact: *https://architecture.louisiana.edu/about-us/contact-us*
Phone: (337) 482-6225
Email: soad@louisiana.edu

COST OF ATTENDANCE:

Tuition & Fees: $10,370 | **Additional Expenses:** $17,374
Total: $27,744

Financial Aid: https://financialaid.louisiana.edu/

ADDITIONAL INFORMATION:

Available Degree(s)

- BS Industrial Design

Scholarships Offered

A variety of scholarships available for resident, nonresident, and international students. Additionally, there are several scholarships available specifically for School of Architecture and Design students.

Summer Programs, Co-ops, Internships

Community job and internship services available.

Special Opportunities, Facilities/Equipment

Study abroad opportunities as well as a trip to Cincinnati to visit General Electric and Kaleidoscope. This hands-on program teaches students how to develop ergonomic, sustainable, human-centered design products in a collaborative and experiential learning environment. Students study visual communication, graphic layout, form development and physical model making, advanced computer modeling, photorealistic rendering, rapid prototyping, and CNC milling.

Notable Alumni

Patrick LeBlanc and Gregory Krikko Obbott

ALABAMA

ARKANSAS

DELAWARE

DISTRICT OF COLUMBIA

FLORIDA

GEORGIA

KENTUCKY

LOUISIANA

MARYLAND

MISSISSIPPI

NORTH CAROLINA

OKLAHOMA

SOUTH CAROLINA

TENNESSEE

TEXAS

VIRGINIA

WEST VIRGINIA

SOUTH

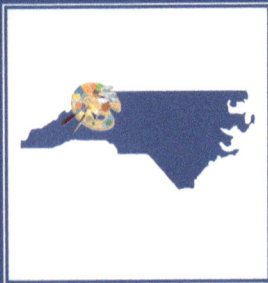

ALABAMA

ARKANSAS

DELAWARE

DISTRICT OF
COLUMBIA

FLORIDA

GEORGIA

KENTUCKY

LOUISIANA

MARYLAND

MISSISSIPPI

NORTH CAROLINA

OKLAHOMA

SOUTH CAROLINA

TENNESSEE

TEXAS

VIRGINIA

WEST VIRGINIA

APPALACHIAN STATE UNIVERSITY

Address: Appalachian State University
Kerr Scott Hall 201
287 Rivers Street
Boone, NC 28608
Website: *https://industrialdesign.appstate.edu/*
Contact: *https://industrialdesign.appstate.edu/contact*
Phone: (828) 262-7333
Email: coreydc@appstate.edu

COST OF ATTENDANCE:

Tuition & Fees: $23,954 | **Additional Expenses:** $16,282
Total: $40,236

Financial Aid: https://financialaid.appstate.edu

ADDITIONAL INFORMATION:

Available Degree(s)

- BS Product Design

Scholarships Offered

Product Design David A. Rigsby Scholarship Endowment, Bill
Hanner Memorial Scholarship, Eric F. Reichard Scholarship in
Technology Automatically considered for ACCESS program and
Appalachian Excellence Scholarship (AES).

Summer Programs, Co-ops, Internships

Through industry collaborations and studio projects, students
are challenged to develop a comprehensive knowledge base
allowing them to compete professionally. Student work has been
recognized and shown at; Greener Gadgets, Dwell® on
Design, Designboom® Mart participants in Copenhagen, High
Point Furniture Market, ICFF and won the national Creative Juice
Completion sponsored by Google®.

Special Opportunities, Facilities/Equipment

"Industrial Designers Society of America (IDSA) - As an extension of
the professional organization IDSA, the club participates in portfolio
reviews, sets up group tours, hosts professional presentations and
travels to district and national conferences. The program facilities
are comprised of dedicated studio space, computer labs and
material exploration facilities supporting a woodworking lab, metal
fabrication lab, plastic working area, ceramics lab, welding facility,
spray booth, CNC lab and rapid prototyping equipment."

Notable Alumni

Dan Millice and Gary E. Wyatt

NORTH CAROLINA STATE UNIVERSITY

Address: NC State University
College of Design
50 Pullen Rd
Raleigh, NC 27695
Website: *https://design.ncsu.edu/industrial-design/*
Contact: *https://design.ncsu.edu/about/contact-us/*
Phone: (919) 515-8302
Email: collegeofdesign@ncsu.edu

COST OF ATTENDANCE:

Tuition & Fees: $32,532.40 | **Additional Expenses:** $11,602
Total: $44,134.80

Financial Aid: https://studentservices.ncsu.edu/your-money/
financial-aid/

ADDITIONAL INFORMATION:

Available Degree(s)

- BID (Bachelors in Industrial Design)
- MID (Masters in Industrial Design)

Scholarships Offered

Program specific scholarships available through the school,
companies, and private donors.

Summer Programs, Co-ops, Internships

Collaborative Research and Design Projects are an integral element
for the Department of Industrial Design. Faculty and students are
exposed to unique client-facing opportunities that challenge them
to develop real-world solutions to actual projects, with major
companies like Coca-Cola, IBM, and John Deere. Many internship
and co-op opportunities.

Special Opportunities, Facilities/Equipment

State of the art facilities include Materials Lab, which includes a
range of equipment, from traditional hand tools to modern CNC
equipment, and allows students to work in wood, plastic, concrete,
and fabric, the William Keating Bayley IT Lab, Exhibition Spaces,
and the Experience Design Lab.

Notable Alumni

Anthony James Barr and Dean Kamen

ALABAMA
ARKANSAS
DELAWARE
DISTRICT OF
COLUMBIA
FLORIDA
GEORGIA
KENTUCKY
LOUISIANA
MARYLAND
MISSISSIPPI
NORTH CAROLINA
OKLAHOMA
SOUTH CAROLINA
TENNESSEE
TEXAS
VIRGINIA
WEST VIRGINIA

SOUTH

ALABAMA
ARKANSAS
DELAWARE
DISTRICT OF COLUMBIA
FLORIDA
GEORGIA
KENTUCKY
LOUISIANA
MARYLAND
MISSISSIPPI
NORTH CAROLINA
OKLAHOMA
SOUTH CAROLINA
TENNESSEE
TEXAS
VIRGINIA
WEST VIRGINIA

UNIVERSITY OF HOUSTON

Address: University of Houston
Gerald D. Hines College of Architecture and Design
4200 Elgin Street, Room 122
Houston, Texas 77204-4000
Website: *https://www.uh.edu/architecture/programs/undergraduate-programs/industrial-design/*
Contact: *https://www.uh.edu/architecture/contacts/*
Phone: (713) 743-3463
Email: archsso@central.uh.edu

COST OF ATTENDANCE:

Tuition & Fees: $22,111 | **Additional Expenses:** $14,211
Total: $36,322

Financial Aid: https://www.uh.edu/financial/

ADDITIONAL INFORMATION:

Available Degree(s)

- BS Industrial Design
- MS Industrial Design

Scholarships Offered

School and department scholarships available.

Summer Programs, Co-ops, Internships

Design Experience Summer program, internships available.

Special Opportunities, Facilities/Equipment

UH has Design/Build Studios, DesignLAB Houston. The College of Architecture and Design provides services through the Computer Lab, Materials Research Collaborative, Jenkins Architecture and Art Library. A premier program at UH, students have unique resources at NASA, Texas Medical Center, and industrial corporations.

The UH program is project-based and studio-centered with top-notch fabrication facilities. The Keeland Design Exploration Laboratory is one of the largest university-based digital fabrication labs in the U.S. The 8,500-sq.ft. building houses state-of-the-art equipment enabling students to design and generate prototypes using 3D software and specialized machinery. Adjacent to the Keeland Laboratory is the new Advanced Media Technology Laboratory for emerging technologies in Texas with cutting-edge advanced digital technologies, including construction robotics, full-scale 3D printing, and augmented/virtual realities.

Notable Alumni

Aubrey Tucker and Mariel Yebra

VIRGINIA POLYTECHNIC INSTITUTE AND STATE UNIVERSITY

Address: School of Architecture + Design (MC0205)
Cowgill Hall, RM 201, Virginia Tech
1325 Perry St, Blacksburg, VA 24061 USA
Website: *https://archdesign.caus.vt.edu/ids/*
Contact: *https://archdesign.caus.vt.edu/ids/contact/*
Phone: (540) 231-5383
Email: mlsulli@vt.edu

COST OF ATTENDANCE:

Tuition & Fees: $33,857 | **Additional Expenses:** $15,446
Total: $49,303

Financial Aid: https://finaid.vt.edu/

ADDITIONAL INFORMATION:

Available Degree(s)

- BS Industrial Design
- BS Packaging Systems Design
- MS Human-Centered Design

Scholarships Offered

Eight ID scholarships offered.

Summer Programs, Co-ops, Internships

The Center for Design Research (CDR) links the academy, industry, and design practice by creating opportunities for collaboration; establishing corporate partnerships and sponsorships; expands capacity by building relationships within the design professions and affiliated industries; initiates collaborative research projects. Summer Academy is designed specifically for incoming freshman and transfer students to come and experience campus life six weeks before the rush of fall.

Special Opportunities, Facilities/Equipment

Study Abroad program. Computer Aided Design, Engineering, and Manufacturing (CAD, CAE, CAM) tools. The BS in Packaging Systems Design combines engineering and sustainable design using materials and biomaterials in packaging for transportation, storage, and product delivery to withstand loads and optimize component interaction.

Notable Alumni

Richard Baker, Jess Cliffe and Michelle Noceto

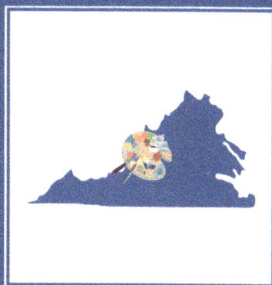

ALABAMA
ARKANSAS
DELAWARE
DISTRICT OF COLUMBIA
FLORIDA
GEORGIA
KENTUCKY
LOUISIANA
MARYLAND
MISSISSIPPI
NORTH CAROLINA
OKLAHOMA
SOUTH CAROLINA
TENNESSEE
TEXAS
VIRGINIA
WEST VIRGINIA

SOUTH

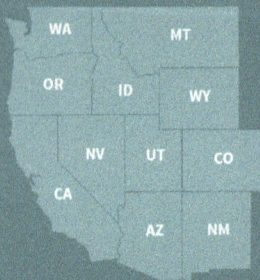

CHAPTER 16
REGION FOUR
WEST

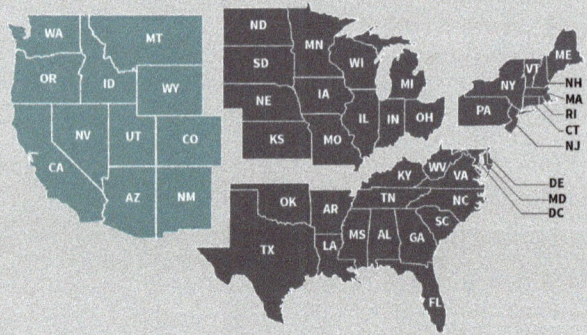

10 *Programs* | **13** *States*

1. *AZ - Arizona State University*
2. *CA - California State University, Long Beach*
3. *CA - San Diego State University*
4. *CA - San Francisco State University*
5. *CA - Stanford University*
6. *OR - University of Oregon*
7. *UT - Brigham Young University*
8. *UT - University of Utah*
9. *WA - University of Washington, Seattle,*
10. *WA - Western Washington University*

INDUSTRIAL DESIGN PROGRAMS

School	Avg. GPA, SAT Evidence-Based Reading Writing (ERW), SAT Math (M), and ACT Composite (C) Early Decision (ED): Yes/No	Admission Statistics	Program(s)
Arizona State University 1151 S. Forest Ave. Tempe, AZ 85281	GPA: N/A SAT (ERW): 550-650 SAT (M): 550-670 ACT (C): 21-28 *Test-optional ED: No	Admit Rate: 88% Undergrad Enrollment: 63,124 Total Enrollment: 74,795	BSD Industrial Design BA Digital Culture, Design MID Industrial Design MSD Industrial Design MS Digital Culture (Extended Reality Technologies) MS IVD Ph.D. Design, Environment and the Arts (Design)
California State University, Long Beach (CSULB) 1250 Bellflower Boulevard, Long Beach, CA 90840	GPA: 3.68 SAT (ERW): 510-620 SAT (M): 510-620 ACT (C): 20-26 ED: No	Admit Rate: 42% Undergrad Enrollment: 34,216 Total Enrollment: 40,069	BS Industrial Design
San Diego State University (SDSU) 5500 Campanile Drive, San Diego, CA 92182	GPA: 3.82 SAT (ERW): 560-660 SAT (M): 560-670 ACT (C): 22-29 ED: No	Admit Rate: 38% Undergrad Enrollment: 30,865 Total Enrollment: 35,732	BA Applied Design, concentrations: Furniture & Woodworking; Metalsmithing MA Applied Design MFA Applied Design
San Francisco State University 1600 Holloway Avenue - Burk Hall 329, San Francisco, CA 94132	GPA: 3.26 SAT (ERW): 470-580 SAT (M): 470-570 ACT (C): 17-23 ED: No	Admit Rate: 84% Undergrad Enrollment: 24,024 Total Enrollment: 27,349	BS Industrial Design MS Design

School	Avg. GPA, SAT Evidence-Based Reading Writing (ERW), SAT Math (M), and ACT Composite (C) Early Decision (ED): Yes/No	Admission Statistics	Program(s)
Stanford University 355 Galvez Street, Stanford, CA 94305	GPA: 3.96 SAT (ERW): 720-770 SAT (M): 750-800 ACT (C): 34-35 ED: No	Admit Rate: 4% Undergrad Enrollment: 7,645 Total Enrollment: 17,680	BS Engineering, concentration: Product Design MS Engineering – Product Design
University of Oregon 5249 University of Oregon, Eugene, OR 97403	GPA: 3.65 SAT (ERW): 550-650 SAT (M): 540-640 ACT (C): 22-29 ED: No	Overall College Admit Rate: 84% Undergrad Enrollment: 18,045 Total Enrollment: 21,752	BFA Product Design MS Sports Product Design
Brigham Young University Brigham Young University, Provo, UT 84602	GPA: 3.86 SAT (ERW): 610-700 SAT (M): 590-710 ACT (C): 26-32 ED: No	Admit Rate: 69% Undergrad Enrollment: 33,365 Total Enrollment: 36,450	BFA Industrial Design BS Manufacturing Engineering
University of Utah 201 S 1460 E, Salt Lake City, UT 84112	GPA: 3.64 SAT (ERW): 590-690 SAT (M): 540-690 ACT (C): 22-30 ED: No	Admit Rate: 84% Undergrad Enrollment: 25,826 Total Enrollment: 34,464	BS Design

WEST

INDUSTRIAL DESIGN PROGRAMS

School	Avg. GPA, SAT Evidence-Based Reading Writing (ERW), SAT Math (M), and ACT Composite (C) Early Decision (ED): Yes/No	Admission Statistics	Program(s)
University of Washington 1400 NE Campus Parkway, Seattle, WA, 98195	GPA: 3.82 SAT (ERW): 590-700 SAT (M): 610-753 ACT (C): 27-33 ED: No	Overall College Admit Rate: 56% Undergrad Enrollment: 32,244 Total Enrollment: 48,149	BDes Industrial Design BDes Interaction Design BDes Visual Communication Design MDes Master of Design
Western Washington University 516 High St, Bellingham, WA 98225	GPA: 3.46 SAT (ERW): 550-650 SAT (M): 530-620 ACT (C): 22-28 ED: No	Admit Rate: 94% Undergrad Enrollment: 14,194 Total Enrollment: 15,197	BS Industrial Design BS Manufacturing Engineering BS Plastics and Composites Engineering

ARIZONA STATE UNIVERSITY

Address: ASU Herberger Institute for Design and the Arts
The Design School
PO Box 871605
Tempe, AZ 85287-1605
Website: *https://design.asu.edu/degree-programs/industrial-design?dept=144305&id=1*
Contact: *https://design.asu.edu/about/contact-us*
Phone: (480) 965-1373
Email: Dosun.Shin@asu.edu

COST OF ATTENDANCE:

Tuition & Fees: $28,800 | **Additional Expenses:** $21,489
Total: $50,289

Financial Aid: https://students.asu.edu/financialaid

ADDITIONAL INFORMATION:

Available Degree(s)

- BSD Industrial Design
- BA Digital Culture (Design)
- MID Industrial Design
- MSD Industrial Design
- MS Digital Culture (Extended Reality Technologies)
- MS IVD (Innovation + Venture Development – Engineering + Business + Design)
- Ph.D. Design, Environment and the Arts (Design)

Scholarships Offered

Ten scholarships offered through the school for both graduate and undergraduate students.

Summer Programs, Co-ops, Internships

Frame a Dream, Green Roofs, The Indigenous Design & Construction Initiative (IDCI)

Special Opportunities, Facilities/Equipment

ASU offers ID students tools and facilities like the Solar Lab, Prototype/Modeling Shop, Design Library, Digital Lab, gallery of Design, ReDesign.School platform, Innovation Space, and The Biomimicry Center, and opportunities to solve real world design issues in projects such as The Interdisciplinary Cluster Competition and the SHADE Solar Decathlon Project

All Herberger Institute students are eligible for complimentary tickets for most events.

Exhibitions at ASU Art Museum Ceramics Research Center, ASU Art Museum, Gallery 100, and Harry Wood Gallery

Notable Alumni

Terry A. Davis, Ed Dwight, and Shon Quannie

CALIFORNIA STATE UNIVERSITY LONG BEACH

Address: CSULB Department of Design
1250 Bellflower Boulevard
Long Beach, CA 90840-5401
Website: *https://www.csulb.edu/design*
Contact: *https://www.csulb.edu/design/contact*
Phone: (562) 985-5089
Email: design@csulb.edu

COST OF ATTENDANCE:

Tuition & Fees: $18,678 | **Additional Expenses:** $17,940
Total: $36,618

Financial Aid: https://www.csulb.edu/financial-aid-and-scholarships

ADDITIONAL INFORMATION:

Available Degree(s)

- BS Industrial Design

Scholarships Offered

The Department of Design receives many exciting scholarship opportunities, including the Nohemi Gonzalez Scholarship for International Study.

Summer Programs, Co-ops, Internships

The Department of Design receives many exciting design opportunities for students including job and competition opportunities, internship opportunities, travel and international exchange opportunities.

Special Opportunities, Facilities/Equipment

The department's academic facilities provide dedicated and controlled access semi-private studio workspaces. These studios are available twenty-four hours a day to all students who have passed portfolio review in the industrial and interior design programs. Each studio workspace provides Ethernet and wireless access to the Internet through the university server.

In addition, several dedicated studios and design laboratories are provided for student use. These facilities include: two Computer Labs, a Multimedia Lab (with large format printing capabilities), a Metal/Plastic and Wood Shop, and three Materials Resource Libraries. The facilities also house a Rapid Prototyping machine (RP) and a Computer Numerical Control machine (CNC), for generating precise models.

Notable Alumni

John Cedarquist, Richard Frinier, and Phillip Lim

ALASKA

ARIZONA

CALIFORNIA

COLORADO

HAWAII

IDAHO

MONTANA

NEVADA

NEW MEXICO

OREGON

UTAH

WASHINGTON

WYOMING

WEST

ALASKA

ARIZONA

CALIFORNIA

COLORADO

HAWAII

IDAHO

MONTANA

NEVADA

NEW MEXICO

OREGON

UTAH

WASHINGTON

WYOMING

SAN DIEGO STATE UNIVERSITY

Address: School of Art + Design
San Diego State University
5500 Campanile Drive
San Diego CA 92182-4805
Website: *https://art.sdsu.edu/programs/applied-design-emphasis/*
Contact: *https://art.sdsu.edu/about-us/our-faculty/*
Phone: (619) 594-6511
Email: artinfo@sdsu.edu

COST OF ATTENDANCE:

Tuition & Fees: $11,880 | **Additional Expenses:** $29,326
Total: $41,206

Financial Aid: https://sacd.sdsu.edu/financial-aid

ADDITIONAL INFORMATION:

Available Degree(s)

- BA Applied Design – Furniture & Woodworking
- BA Applied Design - Metalsmithing
- MA Applied Design
- MFA Applied Design

Scholarships Offered

School, external, and design department scholarships available.

Summer Programs, Co-ops, Internships

Summer fellowships available: Penland School of Craft, Arrowmont School of Arts and Crafts, Haystack Mountain School of Crafts

Special Opportunities, Facilities/Equipment

Visiting artists, study abroad, state of the art facilities, including ceramics studios, wood shop, and metal shop.

Notable Alumni

Amy Devers and Nik Ingersöll.

SAN FRANCISCO STATE UNIVERSITY

Address: San Francisco State University
College of Liberal & Creative Arts School of Design
Fine Arts Room 121
1600 Holloway Avenue
San Francisco, CA 94132
Website: *https://design.sfsu.edu/bachelor-science-industrial-design*
Contact: *https://design.sfsu.edu/contact*
Phone: (415) 338-2211
Email: design@sfsu.edu

COST OF ATTENDANCE:

Tuition & Fees: $19,184 | **Additional Expenses:** $19,065
Total: $38,249

Financial Aid: https://financialaid.sfsu.edu/

ADDITIONAL INFORMATION:

Available Degree(s)

- BS Industrial Design
- MS Design

Scholarships Offered

Four targeted major scholarships as well as institutional options.

Summer Programs, Co-ops, Internships

The School of Design offers opportunities for internship credit through our DES 576 class.

Special Opportunities, Facilities/Equipment

We offer a wide range of design experiences for students including large format printing, letterpress printing, bookbinding, 3D printing, rapid prototyping, full wood and metal shops, as well as interactive media including AR and VR.

SF State Scholars 4+1 – Pathway to an MA in Design graduate degree

Study abroad partner university - The Pontificia Universidad Católica de Chile Santiago, Chile

Notable Alumni

Jack O'Neill

ALASKA

ARIZONA

CALIFORNIA

COLORADO

HAWAII

IDAHO

MONTANA

NEVADA

NEW MEXICO

OREGON

UTAH

WASHINGTON

WYOMING

WEST

ALASKA

ARIZONA

CALIFORNIA

COLORADO

HAWAII

IDAHO

MONTANA

NEVADA

NEW MEXICO

OREGON

UTAH

WASHINGTON

WYOMING

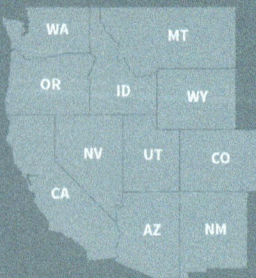

STANFORD UNIVERSITY

Address: Address: Stanford Engineering
475 Via Ortega
Stanford, CA 94305
Website: *https://majors.stanford.edu/product-design*
Contact: *https://engineering.stanford.edu/contact-us*
Phone: (650) 723-2091
Email: wburnett@stanford.edu

COST OF ATTENDANCE:

Tuition & Fees: $56,169 | **Additional Expenses:** $22,110
Total: $77,279

Financial Aid: https://financialaid.stanford.edu/

ADDITIONAL INFORMATION:

Available Degree(s)

- BS Engineering - Product Design
- MS Engineering – Product Design

Scholarships Offered

Numerous scholarship opportunities through school and Engineering Dept.

Summer Programs, Co-ops, Internships

Multiple resources for internships and career opportunities.

Global Engineering Program (GEP) Internship – work with innovative companies that pair with Stanford to utilize your engineering skills abroad.

Chinese Undergraduate Visiting Research (UGVR)

Special Opportunities, Facilities/Equipment

Product Design program is a sub-specialty of Mechanical Engineering and offers over 50 institutes, labs, and centers as part of the college of engineering.

Notable Alumni

Andy Bechtolshelm and Edith Head.

UNIVERSITY OF OREGON

Address: School of Art + Design
Department of Product Design
5282 University of Oregon
Eugene, OR 97403-5282
Office: 254 Lawrence Hall
Website: *https://artdesign.uoregon.edu/pd*
Contact: *https://artdesign.uoregon.edu/pd/contact*
Phone: (541) 346-3610
Email: artdesign@uoregon.edu

COST OF ATTENDANCE:

Tuition & Fees: $42,801 | **Additional Expenses:** $16,105
Total: $58,906

Financial Aid: https://financialaid.uoregon.edu/

ADDITIONAL INFORMATION:

Available Degree(s)

- BFA Product Design
- MS Sports Product Design

Scholarships Offered

More than 110 department scholarships available.

Summer Programs, Co-ops, Internships

Internships and career services available.

Special Opportunities, Facilities/Equipment

Product Design Polymer Lab, wood shop, studios, fab lab, 3D printer, and more. We use woodworking tools, steel fabrication methods, ceramic and plastics molding, and other hand skills alongside high-tech 3-D rendering, cutting, and printing. Study abroad program. Product of Eugene-A partnership between Lane Arts Council and the Department of Product Design, this program offers middle and high school students apprenticeship opportunities in graphic, digital, and physical design. UO offers faculty led global education programs. Explore Global Education Oregon (GEO)

Notable Alumni

Tinker Hatfield

ALASKA

ARIZONA

CALIFORNIA

COLORADO

HAWAII

IDAHO

MONTANA

NEVADA

NEW MEXICO

OREGON

UTAH

WASHINGTON

WYOMING

WEST

ALASKA

ARIZONA

CALIFORNIA

COLORADO

HAWAII

IDAHO

MONTANA

NEVADA

NEW MEXICO

OREGON

UTAH

WASHINGTON

WYOMING

BRIGHAM YOUNG UNIVERSITY

Address: 265 CTB, Brigham Young University
Provo, UT 84602
Website: *https://sot.byu.edu/industrial-design*
Contact: *https://id.byu.edu/*
Phone: (801) 422-6300
Email: sot_sec@byu.edu

COST OF ATTENDANCE:

Tuition & Fees: $12,240 | **Additional Expenses:** $14,036
Total: $26,276

Financial Aid: https://enrollment.byu.edu/financial-aid

ADDITIONAL INFORMATION:

Available Degree(s)

- BFA Industrial Design
- BS Manufacturing Engineering

Scholarships Offered

BYU supports students in applying for several national and international scholarships including the Rhodes Scholar program, the Marshall Scholarship, the Truman Scholarship, the Gates Cambridge Scholarship, and the Fulbright Student Program. Departmental scholarships also available.

Summer Programs, Co-ops, Internships

Domestic and international internships available.

Special Opportunities, Facilities/Equipment

Students learn traditional skills of drawing and model making as well as computer modeling, rendering, and animation. They develop these skills by working on mentored projects sponsored by outside industry partners.

Notable Alumni

Philio Farnsworth and Mark Rober

UNIVERSITY OF UTAH

Address: University of Utah
College of Architecture & Planning
375 South 1530 East AAC 235
Salt Lake City, UT 84103
Website: *https://www.uofu.design/*
Contact: *https://www.uofu.design/contact-us*
Phone: (801) 581-8254
Email: eataata@arch.utah.edu

COST OF ATTENDANCE:

Tuition & Fees: $29,516 | **Additional Expenses:** $14,327
Total: $43,843

Financial Aid: https://financialaid.utah.edu/

ADDITIONAL INFORMATION:

Available Degree(s)

- BS Design

Scholarships Offered

University scholarships available.

Summer Programs, Co-ops, Internships

MDD Internship Requirement – 120 hours

Design office, study abroad, teaching assistant, non-profit, government, or policy position

Special Opportunities, Facilities/Equipment

Multiple design studios, annual camping trip. Multiple machine shops and labs on campus.

Notable Alumni

Mary Blade and Mark W. Fuller

ALASKA

ARIZONA

CALIFORNIA

COLORADO

HAWAII

IDAHO

MONTANA

NEVADA

NEW MEXICO

OREGON

UTAH

WASHINGTON

WYOMING

WEST

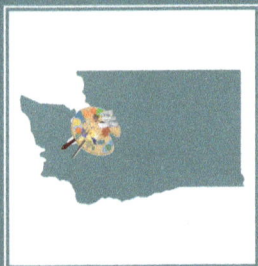

ALASKA

ARIZONA

CALIFORNIA

COLORADO

HAWAII

IDAHO

MONTANA

NEVADA

NEW MEXICO

OREGON

UTAH

WASHINGTON

WYOMING

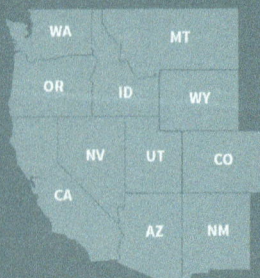

UNIVERSITY OF WASHINGTON, SEATTLE

Address: School of Art + Art History + Design
University of Washington
Box 353440
Seattle, WA 98195-3440
Website: *https://art.washington.edu/design/industrial-design-bdes*
Contact: *https://art.washington.edu/contact*
Phone: (206) 543-0970
Email: gradart@uw.edu

COST OF ATTENDANCE:

Tuition & Fees: $40,714 | **Additional Expenses:** $18,713
Total: $59,427

Financial Aid: https://www.washington.edu/financialaid/

ADDITIONAL INFORMATION:

Available Degree(s)

- BDes Industrial Design
- BDes Interaction Design
- BDes Visual Communication Design
- MDes Master of Design

Scholarships Offered

Three department specific scholarships available.

Crabby Beach Foundation or Kathryn Hinckley-Martin Scholarship in Art - $5,000

Graduating with Excellence Awards

Pilchuck Glass School scholarship covering summer program

Summer Programs, Co-ops, Internships

Internships, fellowships, volunteer, and career opportunities available.

Special Opportunities, Facilities/Equipment

Study abroad programs and an exploration seminar available. Numerous labs, shops, and studios with state of the art equipment for modeling, fabrication, printing, etc available to design majors.

UW's curriculum includes ideation, scenario-building, concept selection, refinement, detailing, model-making, prototyping, testing, refining, and production as well as delivering presentations, participating in collaborative problem-solving, and showing artwork at the Parnassus Art Gallery.

Notable Alumni

George Nakashima and Norie Sato

WESTERN WASHINGTON UNIVERSITY

Address: Western Washington University
Engineering & Design Department
College of Science & Engineering
Ross Engineering Technology (ET 204)
516 High Street, Bellingham, WA 9822
Website: *https://engineeringdesign.wwu.edu/industrial-design*
Contact: *https://www.wwu.edu/wwucontact/*
Phone: (360) 650-3380
Email: lisa.ochs@wwu.edu

COST OF ATTENDANCE:

Tuition & Fees: $26,611 | **Additional Expenses:** $17,563
Total: $44,174

Financial Aid: https://www.finaid.wwu.edu/

ADDITIONAL INFORMATION:

Available Degree(s)

- BS Industrial Design
- BS Manufacturing Engineering
- BS Plastics and Composites Engineering
- Material Science Minor
- Embedded Systems Minor
- User Experience Minor

Scholarships Offered

The Engineering & Design Department offers a number of scholarships every year.

Jarvis Memorial Summer Research Award

Summer Programs, Co-ops, Internships

Internships and employment program available.

Special Opportunities, Facilities/Equipment

Industrial design students are taught problem-solving methodologies, marketing principles, usability research, drawing skills, three-dimensional model-making techniques, materials, form theory, color application, manufacturing processes, ergonomics, and design principles, with access to amazing manufacturing facilities: CNC, waterjet cutters, laser cutter, FDM 3D printing, composite labs, injection molds, extruders, milling machines, welding, CNC routers, paint booths and all the standard shop equipment that you need to make anything you can imagine.

Material Science Minor

Embedded Systems Minor

User Experience Minor

Notable Alumni

Charles Eames and Jolee Evans

ALASKA

ARIZONA

CALIFORNIA

COLORADO

HAWAII

IDAHO

MONTANA

NEVADA

NEW MEXICO

OREGON

UTAH

WASHINGTON

WYOMING

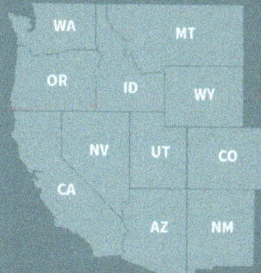

WEST

CHAPTER 17

INDUSTRIAL & PRODUCT DESIGN SCHOOLS ALPHABETIZED BY CITY & STATE

School	City	State
Auburn University	Auburn	Alabama
Arizona State University	Tempe	Arizona
California State University, Long Beach	Long Beach	California
San Diego State University	San Diego	California
San Francisco State University	San Francisco	California
Stanford University	Stanford	California
Georgia Institute of Technology	Atlanta	Georgia
Savannah College of Art and Design	Savannah	Georgia
University of Illinois Urbana-Champaign (UIUC)	Champaign	Illinois
University of Illinois, Chicago	Chicago	Illinois
University of Notre Dame	Notre Dame	Indiana
Purdue University	West Lafayette	Indiana
Iowa State University	Ames	Iowa
University of Louisiana, Lafayette	Lafayette	Louisiana
Massachusetts College of Art & Design	Boston	Massachusetts
Wentworth Institute of Technology	Boston	Massachusetts
Lawrence Technological University	Southfield	Michigan
University of Minnesota, Twin Cities	Minneapolis	Minnesota
Montclair State University	Montclair	New Jersey
Kean University	Union	New Jersey
Pratt Institute	Brooklyn	New York
Parsons School of Design	New York	New York
Rochester Institute of Technology	Rochester	New York
Appalachian State University	Boone	North Carolina
North Carolina State University (NC State)	Raleigh	North Carolina
Cedarville University	Cedarville	Ohio
University of Cincinnati	Cincinnati	Ohio
Ohio State University	Columbus	Ohio
University of Oregon	Eugene	Oregon
Drexel University	Philadelphia	Pennsylvania
Carnegie Mellon University	Pittsburgh	Pennsylvania
Swarthmore College	Swarthmore	Pennsylvania
Pennsylvania College of Technology	Williamsport	Pennsylvania
Rhode Island School of Design	Providence	Rhode Island
The University of Houston	Houston	Texas

School	City	State
Brigham Young University	Provo	Utah
University of Utah	Salt Lake City	Utah
Virginia Polytechnic Institute and State University	Blacksburg	Virginia
Western Washington University	Bellingham	Washington
University of Washington	Seattle	Washington
University of Wisconsin, Stout	Menomonie	Wisconsin

CHAPTER 18

INDUSTRIAL & PRODUCT DESIGN PROGRAMS BY AVERAGE GPA & TEST SCORES

INDUSTRIAL & PRODUCT DESIGN PROGRAMS BY AVERAGE GPA

School	Avg. GPA
San Francisco State University	3.26
Western Washington University	3.46
Lawrence Technological University	3.5
Savannah College of Art and Design	3.6
University of Oregon	3.65
Purdue University	3.67
Rochester Institute of Technology	3.7
University of Cincinnati	3.7
Iowa State University	3.71
The University of Houston	3.73
North Carolina State University (NC State)	3.8
Pratt Institute	3.82
University of Washington	3.82
Carnegie Mellon University	3.85
Cedarville University	3.91
Virginia Polytechnic Institute and State University	3.96
Auburn University	3.97
Appalachian State University	3.98
Georgia Institute of Technology	4.09
University of Minnesota, Twin Cities	3.53
University of Utah	3.64
California State University, Long Beach	3.68
San Diego State University	3.82
Brigham Young University	3.86
Stanford University	3.96
Arizona State University	N/A
Drexel University	N/A
Kean University	N/A
Massachusetts College of Art & Design	N/A
Montclair State University	N/A
Ohio State University	N/A
Parsons School of Design	N/A
Pennsylvania College of Technology	N/A
Rhode Island School of Design	N/A
Swarthmore College	N/A
University of Illinois Urbana-Champaign (UIUC)	N/A

University of Illinois, Chicago	N/A
University of Louisiana, Lafayette	N/A
University of Notre Dame	N/A
University of Wisconsin, Stout	N/A
Wentworth Institute of Technology	N/A

INDUSTRIAL & PRODUCT DESIGN PROGRAMS BY AVERAGE SAT

School	Avg. SAT
Kean University	460-550 (ERW) 460-550 (M)
San Francisco State University	470-580 (ERW) 470-570 (M)
Iowa State University	480-630 (ERW) 530-680 (M)
Montclair State University	500-600 (ERW) 510-610 (M) *Test optional
Lawrence Technological University	500-620 (ERW) 520-660 (M)
University of Illinois, Chicago	510-610 (ERW) 520-640 (M)
University of Louisiana, Lafayette	510-620 (ERW) 490-590 (M)
California State University, Long Beach	510-620 (ERW) 510-620 (M)
University of Minnesota, Twin Cities	530-620 (ERW) 520-640 (M) *Test-optional
Wentworth Institute of Technology	540-630 (ERW) 550-650 (M)
Appalachian State University	540-630 (ERW) 530-610 (M)
Savannah College of Art and Design	540-640 (ERW) 500-600 (M)
Western Washington University	550-650 (ERW) 530-620 (M)
University of Oregon	550-650 (ERW) 540-640 (M)
Arizona State University	550-650 (ERW) 550-670 (M) *Test-optional
The University of Houston	560-650 (ERW) 560-660 (M)
University of Cincinnati	560-650 (ERW) 560-680 (M)
San Diego State University	560-660 (ERW) 560-670 (M)
Pratt Institute	570-660 (ERW) 550-680 (M)
Cedarville University	570-680 (ERW) 540-670 (M)
Parsons School of Design	580-680 (ERW) 560-680 (M)
Auburn University	590-650 (ERW) 580-680 (M)
Virginia Polytechnic Institute and State University	590-680 (ERW) 580-690 (M)
Drexel University	590-680 (ERW) 590-700 (M)
Purdue University	590-690 (ERW) 600-740 (M)
Ohio State University	590-690 (ERW) 620-740 (M)

School	Avg. GPA
University of Utah	590-690 (ERW) 540-690 (M)
University of Washington	590-700 (ERW) 610-753 (M)
University of Illinois Urbana-Champaign (UIUC)	590-700 (ERW) 620-770 (M)
Rochester Institute of Technology	600-690 (ERW) 620-730 (M)
Rhode Island School of Design	610-700 (ERW) 640-770 (M)
Brigham Young University	610-700 (ERW) 590-710 (M)
North Carolina State University (NC State)	620-690 (ERW) 630-730 (M)
Georgia Institute of Technology	670-740 (ERW) 700-790 (M)
Swarthmore College	690-750 (ERW) 705-790 (M)
University of Notre Dame	690-760 (ERW) 710-790 (M)
Carnegie Mellon University	700-760 (ERW) 760-800 (M)
Stanford University	720-770 (ERW) 750-800 (M)
University of Wisconsin, Stout	N/A
Massachusetts College of Art & Design	N/A *Test optional
Pennsylvania College of Technology	N/A *Test optional

INDUSTRIAL & PRODUCT DESIGN PROGRAMS BY AVERAGE ACT

School	Avg. ACT C
Kean University	16-22
San Francisco State University	17-23
University of Wisconsin, Stout	20-25
California State University, Long Beach	20-26
University of Louisiana, Lafayette	20-26
Savannah College of Art and Design	20-27
University of Minnesota, Twin Cities	21-26 *Test-optional
Montclair State University	21-28 *Test optional
Iowa State University	21-28
Arizona State University	21-28 *Test-optional
Lawrence Technological University	21-29
University of Illinois, Chicago	21-29
Appalachian State University	22-27
Western Washington University	22-28
The University of Houston	22-28
San Diego State University	22-29
University of Oregon	22-29
University of Utah	22-30
Wentworth Institute of Technology	23-28

School	Avg. ACT C
University of Cincinnati	23-29
Cedarville University	23-30
Auburn University	24-30
Pratt Institute	25-30
Drexel University	25-31
Virginia Polytechnic Institute and State University	25-31
Purdue University	25-33
Parsons School of Design	26-30
Brigham Young University	26-32
Ohio State University	26-32
North Carolina State University (NC State)	27-32
Rhode Island School of Design	27-32
University of Illinois Urbana-Champaign (UIUC)	27-33
University of Washington	27-33
Rochester Institute of Technology	28-33
Swarthmore College	31-34
Georgia Institute of Technology	31-35
University of Notre Dame	32-35
Carnegie Mellon University	33-35
Stanford University	34-35
Massachusetts College of Art & Design	N/A *Test optional
Pennsylvania College of Technology	N/A *Test optional

CHAPTER 19

TOP 20 GRADUATE SCHOOLS FOR SCULPTURE

S/N	School
1	Virginia Commonwealth University
2	UCLA
3	Yale University
4	Rhode Island School of Design
5	School of the Art Institute Chicago
6	Maryland Institute College of Art
7	University of Texas, Austin
8	Bard College
9	California Institute of the Arts
10	Columbia University
11	Cranbrook Academy of Art
12	New York University
13	Massachusetts Institute of Technology
14	CUNY - Hunter College
15	Pratt Institute
16	Carnegie Mellon University
17	Stanford University
18	Temple University
19	University of Georgia
20	Boston University

CHAPTER 20

TOP PROGRAMS IN JEWELRY, METAL ARTS, & GLASS BLOWING

TOP 40 PROGRAMS IN JEWELRY AND METAL ARTS

California

Academy of Art University, SF – AA, BFA, MA, MFA – Jewelry & Metal Arts

California College of the Arts – BFA Jewelry & Metal Arts

Cal State Long Beach – BFA Metal & Jewelry

Humboldt State University -BFA Jewelry & Small Metals

San Diego State University – MFA Jewelry & Metalsmithing

Colorado

Colorado State University – BFA in Art, Metalsmithing

Georgia

Savannah Col. of Art & Design – BFA Jewelry Design, BFA Metals & Jewelry

Illinois

Illinois State University – BFA Wood & Metals

Northern Illinois University – BFA Metalwork, Jewelry Design, & Digital Fabrication

Southern Illinois University – BFA, MFA in Jewelry & Metalsmithing

Indiana

Ball State University - BFA in Art, focus in Metal

Indiana University at Bloomington – BFA Studio Art, focus - Metals + Jewelry

Kansas

University of Kansas – BFA Metalsmithing/Jewelry

Kentucky

Eastern Kentucky University – BFA Jewelry and Metals

Maine

Maine College of Art – BFA Metalsmithing/Jewelry

Michigan

Cranbrook Academy of Art – MFA Metalsmithing

Grand Valley State University – BFA Jewelry and Metalsmithing

Kendall College of Art & Design – BFA Metals and Jewelry Design

Univ. of Michigan, Ann Arbor – BFA Metalsmithing & Jewelry focus

Massachusetts

Mass. College of Art & Design – BFA Jewelry & Metalsmithing

New York

Fashion Inst. of Technology – AAS Jewelry Design

Rochester Inst. of Technology – BFA Studio Arts, Jewelry Design & Metalsmithing option

SUNY Buffalo – BFA Metals/Jewelry

SUNY New Paltz – BA/BFA Studio Arts in Metal

Syracuse University – BFA Studio Arts, emphasis in Jewelry & Metalsmithing

North Carolina

East Carolina University – BFA/MFA Metal Design

Ohio

Bowling Green State University - BFA, MFA focus Jewelry/Metal

Miami University – BFA Metals & Jewelry Design

University of Akron – BFA Jewelry & Metalsmithing

Oregon

University of Oregon – BFA Jewelry & Metalsmithing

Pennsylvania

Arcadia University – BFA in Art, concentration in Metals and Jewelry

Edinboro University – BFA/MFA Jewelry and Metalsmithing

Temple University – BFA in Metals/Jewelry/CAD-CAM

Rhode Island

Rhode Island School of Design – BFA Jewelry + Metalsmithing

Texas

Texas Tech – BFA in Art, emphasis in Jewelry Design & Metalsmithing

University of North Texas – BFA Metalsmithing & Jewelry

Virginia

Radford University – BFA Jewelry and Metalworking

Virginia Commonwealth University – BFA, MFA – Metal/Jewelry

Washington

Central Washington University – BA Art + Design, Studio Area - Jewelry/Metalsmithing

Wisconsin

University of Wisconsin, Milwaukee – BFA Jewelry & Metalsmithing

TOP 20 COLLEGES FOR GLASS BLOWING

Alabama

University of South Alabama – BFA Studio Art, Glass

California

California College of the Arts – BFA Glass

Central College – BFA Glass Blowing

Florida

Jacksonville University – BFA Object Design (Glass)

Illinois

Illinois State University, BFA Studio Arts, focus in Glass

Southern Illinois University – BFA, MFA in Glass

Indiana

Ball State University – BFA in Art, focus in Glass

Louisiana

Tulane University – BFA Studio Art, discipline in Glass

Massachusetts

Massachusetts College of Art and Design – BFA, MFA in Glass

New York

Alfred University – the only ABET Accredited Glass Engineering program in the US

Hartwick College – BA in Art, focus in Glass

Rochester Institute of Technology – BFA Studio Art, Glass option; MFA Glass

Ohio

Bowling Green State University – BA/BFA/MFA in Studio Art, focus in Glass

Ohio State University – BA/BFA/MFA Studio Art, area - Glass

Rhode Island

Rhode Island School of Design – BFA/MFA Glass

Pennsylvania

Temple University – BFA/MFA in Glass

Texas

University of Texas, Arlington – BFA in Glass

Virginia

Virginia Commonwealth University – BFA, MFA – Glass

Washington

University of Washington – BA/MFA in Art - 3D4M Ceramics + Glass + Sculpture

Wisconsin

University of Wisconsin, Madison – BFA in Art, area Glass and Neon

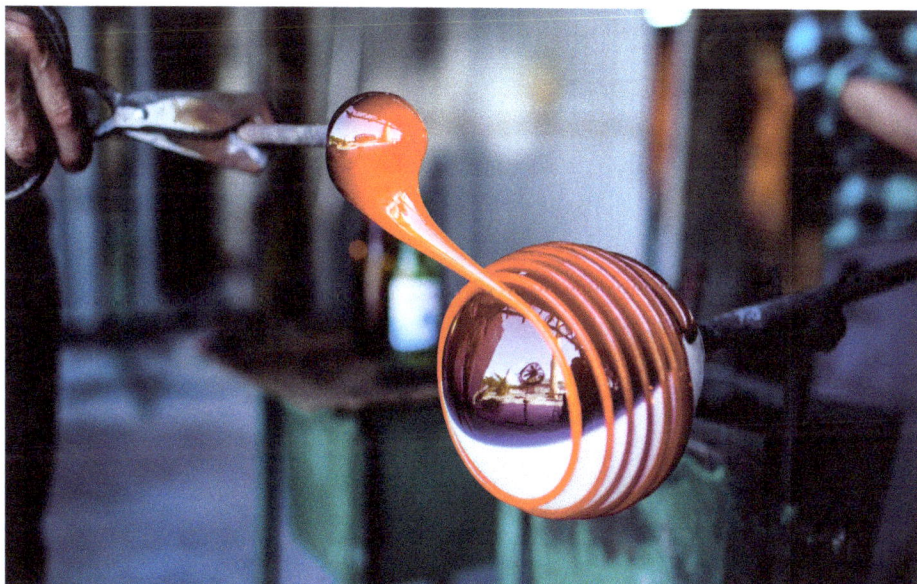

CHAPTER 21

ACT AND SAT
CONCORDANCE TABLE

ACT	SAT	SAT Range
36	1590	1570–1600
35	1540	1530–1560
34	1500	1490–1520
33	1460	1450–1480
32	1430	1420–1440
31	1400	1390–1410
30	1370	1360–1380
29	1340	1330–1350
28	1310	1300–1320
27	1280	1260–1290
26	1240	1230–1250
25	1210	1200–1220
24	1180	1160–1190
23	1140	1130–1150
22	1110	1100–1120
21	1080	1060–1090
20	1040	1030–1050
19	1010	990–1020
18	970	960–980
17	930	920–950
16	890	880–910
15	850	830–870
14	800	780–820
13	760	730–770
12	710	690–720
11	670	650–680
10	630	620–640
9	590	590–610

Source: https://www.act.org/content/dam/act/unsecured/documents/ACT-SAT-Concordance-Information.pdf

JOURNEY TO ART, DANCE, MUSIC, THEATRE, FILM, AND FASHION SERIES

JOURNEY TO

Fashion Design

COLLEGE ADMISSIONS & PROFILES

RACHEL A. WINSTON, PH.D.

JOURNEY TO

Fashion Merchandising

COLLEGE ADMISSIONS & PROFILES

RACHEL A. WINSTON, PH.D.

JOURNEY TO

Costume Design & Technical Theatre

COLLEGE ADMISSIONS & PROFILES

RACHEL A. WINSTON, PH.D.

JOURNEY TO

Theatre and the Dramatic Arts

COLLEGE ADMISSIONS & PROFILES

RACHEL A. WINSTON, PH.D.

223

JOURNEY TO
Musical
Theatre
COLLEGE ADMISSIONS & PROFILES

RACHEL A. WINSTON, PH.D.

JOURNEY TO
Architecture
COLLEGE ADMISSIONS & PROFILES

RACHEL A. WINSTON, PH.D.

JOURNEY TO
Photography
COLLEGE ADMISSIONS & PROFILES
FASHION, SPORTS, ART, TRAVEL, & JOURNALISM

RACHEL A. WINSTON, PH.D.

JOURNEY TO
Illustration
and
Comic Book Design
COLLEGE ADMISSIONS & PROFILES

RACHEL A. WINSTON, PH.D.

JOURNEY TO
Drawing
and
Painting
COLLEGE ADMISSIONS & PROFILES

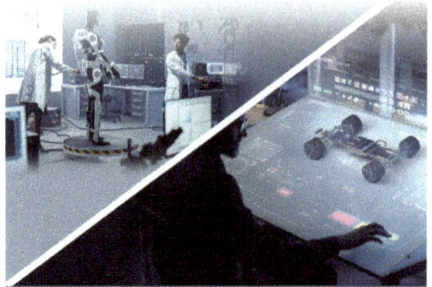

RACHEL A. WINSTON, PH.D.

JOURNEY TO
Industrial &
Product Design
COLLEGE ADMISSIONS & PROFILES

RACHEL A. WINSTON, PH.D.

JOURNEY TO
3-D
Art & Design
COLLEGE ADMISSIONS & PROFILES
SCULPTURE, CERAMICS,
GLASS, & JEWELRY DESIGN

RACHEL A. WINSTON, PH.D.

JOURNEY TO
Graphic Design,
Advertising,
& Public Relations
COLLEGE ADMISSIONS & PROFILES

RACHEL A. WINSTON, PH.D.

JOURNEY TO
Film Directing & Production

COLLEGE ADMISSIONS & PROFILES
FILM, TELEVISION, & MEDIA ARTS

RACHEL A. WINSTON, PH.D.

JOURNEY TO
Screenwriting & Film and Cinema Studies

COLLEGE ADMISSIONS & PROFILES
WRITING, CULTURE, HISTORY, & CRITICAL ANALYSIS

RACHEL A. WINSTON, PH.D.

JOURNEY TO
Newspaper, Radio, & Broadcast Journalism

COLLEGE ADMISSIONS & PROFILES
TELEVISION, RADIO, PRINT & NEW MEDIA

RACHEL A. WINSTON, PH.D.

JOURNEY TO
Dance

COLLEGE ADMISSIONS & PROFILES
BALLET, CONTEMPORARY, MODERN, JAZZ,
TAP, HIP HOP, THEATRICAL, & BALLROOM

RACHEL A. WINSTON, PH.D.

JOURNEY TO
Psychology
COLLEGE ADMISSIONS & PROFILES
CLINICAL, COUNSELING, SPORTS, & EDUCATIONAL

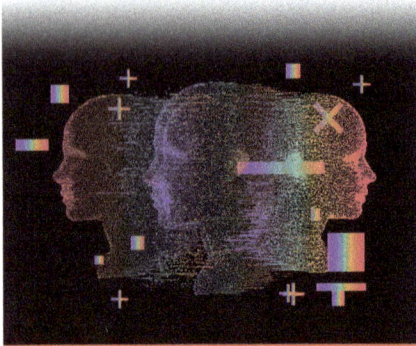

RACHEL A. WINSTON, PH.D.

JOURNEY TO
Forensic Psych.,
Crime Scene,
& Cybercrime
COLLEGE ADMISSIONS & PROFILES

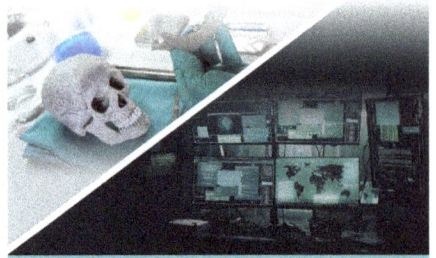

RACHEL A. WINSTON, PH.D.

JOURNEY TO
Animation &
Game Design
COLLEGE ADMISSIONS & PROFILES

RACHEL A. WINSTON, PH.D.

JOURNEY TO
Law &
Criminal Justice
COLLEGE ADMISSIONS & PROFILES

RACHEL A. WINSTON, PH.D.

Live your dreams today remembering that discipline is the bridge between dreams and achievement!

"We believe in the American Dream that all people rich or poor can go as far in life as their talents and persistence will take them."

– Lizard Publishing Vision

At Lizard, we help you make your dreams come true.

CONTACT INFORMATION

Phone: 949-833-7706

E-mail: collegeguide@yahoo.com

Website: collegelizard.com and Lizard-publishing.com

COMPREHENSIVE HEALTH CARE SERIES

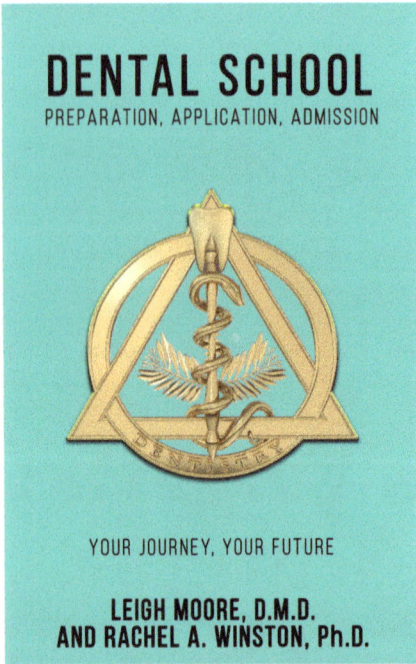

DENTAL SCHOOL
PREPARATION, APPLICATION, ADMISSION

YOUR JOURNEY, YOUR FUTURE

LEIGH MOORE, D.M.D.
AND RACHEL A. WINSTON, Ph.D.

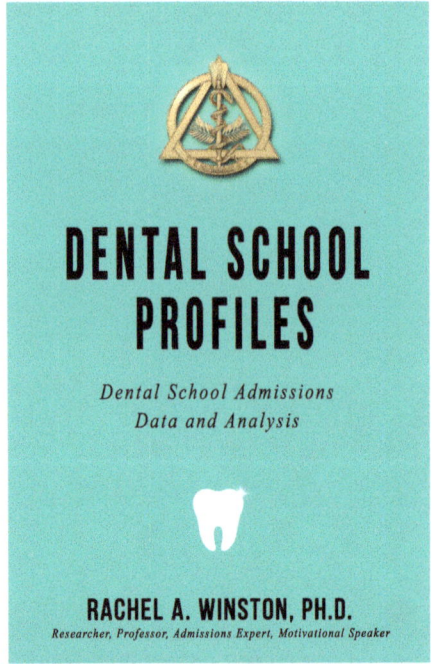

DENTAL SCHOOL PROFILES

Dental School Admissions Data and Analysis

RACHEL A. WINSTON, PH.D.
Researcher, Professor, Admissions Expert, Motivational Speaker

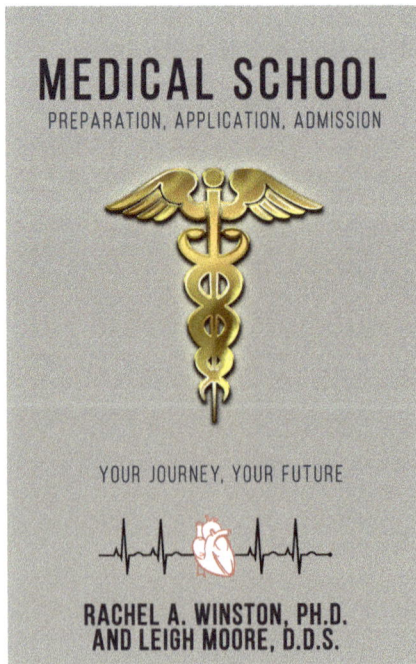

MEDICAL SCHOOL
PREPARATION, APPLICATION, ADMISSION

YOUR JOURNEY, YOUR FUTURE

RACHEL A. WINSTON, PH.D.
AND LEIGH MOORE, D.D.S.

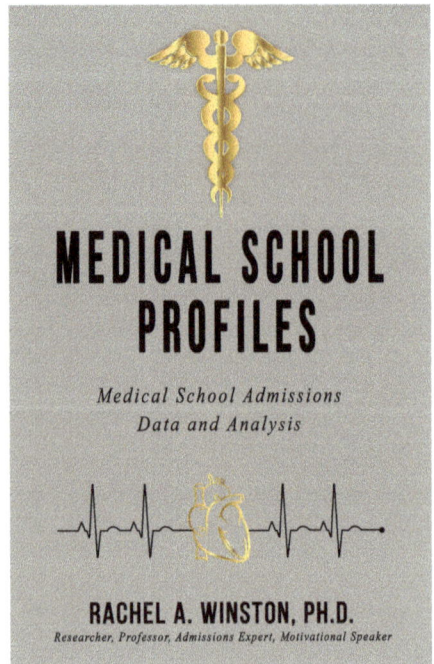

MEDICAL SCHOOL PROFILES

Medical School Admissions Data and Analysis

RACHEL A. WINSTON, PH.D.
Researcher, Professor, Admissions Expert, Motivational Speaker

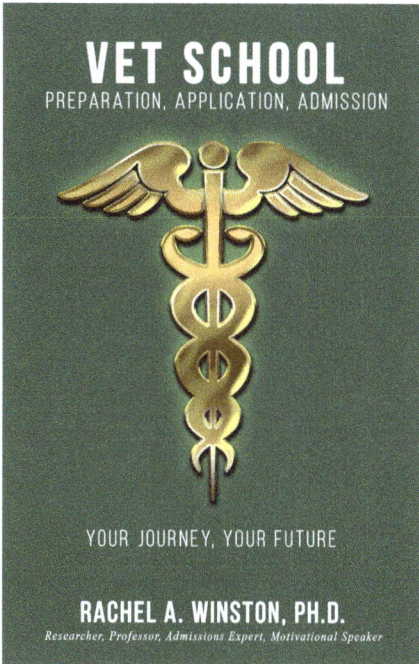

VET SCHOOL
PREPARATION, APPLICATION, ADMISSION

YOUR JOURNEY, YOUR FUTURE

RACHEL A. WINSTON, PH.D.
Researcher, Professor, Admissions Expert, Motivational Speaker

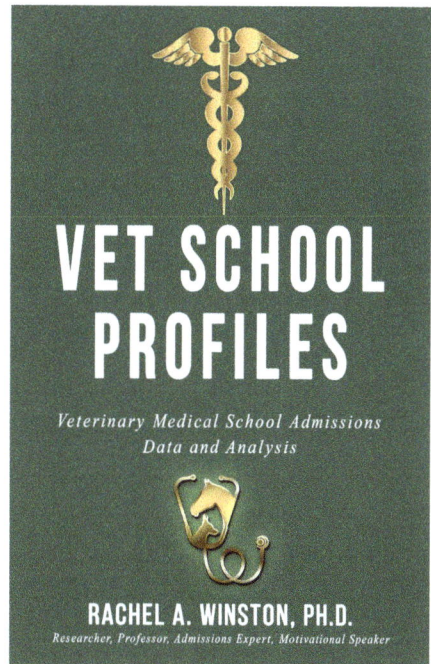

VET SCHOOL PROFILES

Veterinary Medical School Admissions Data and Analysis

RACHEL A. WINSTON, PH.D.
Researcher, Professor, Admissions Expert, Motivational Speaker

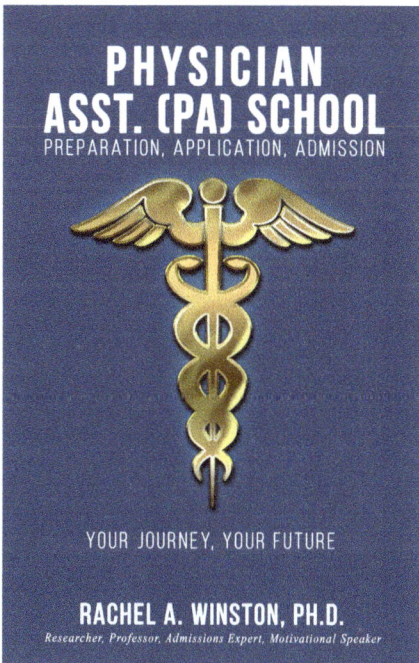

PHYSICIAN ASST. (PA) SCHOOL
PREPARATION, APPLICATION, ADMISSION

YOUR JOURNEY, YOUR FUTURE

RACHEL A. WINSTON, PH.D.
Researcher, Professor, Admissions Expert, Motivational Speaker

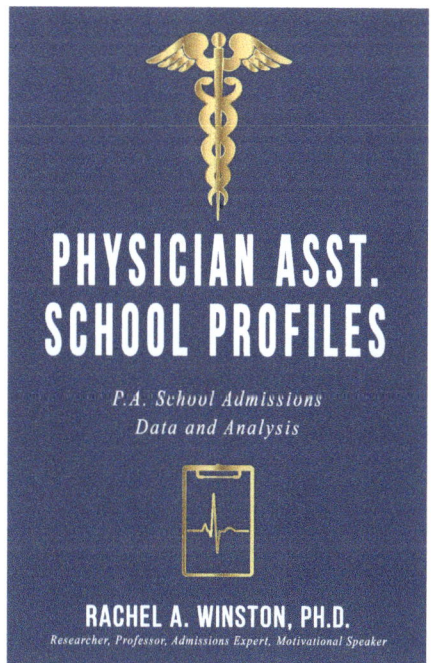

PHYSICIAN ASST. SCHOOL PROFILES

P.A. School Admissions Data and Analysis

RACHEL A. WINSTON, PH.D.
Researcher, Professor, Admissions Expert, Motivational Speaker

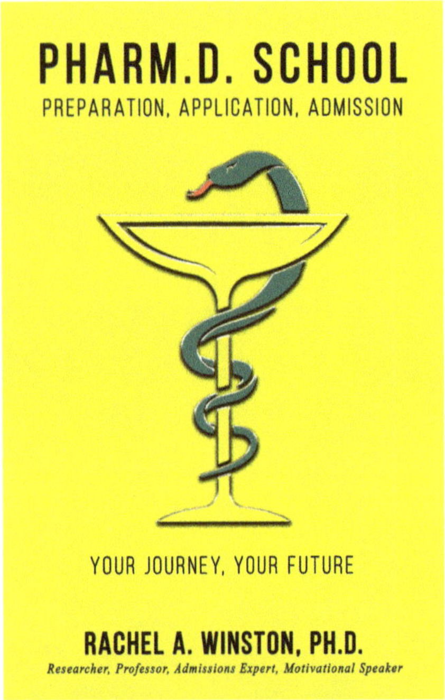

PHARM.D. SCHOOL
PREPARATION, APPLICATION, ADMISSION

YOUR JOURNEY, YOUR FUTURE

RACHEL A. WINSTON, PH.D.
Researcher, Professor, Admissions Expert, Motivational Speaker

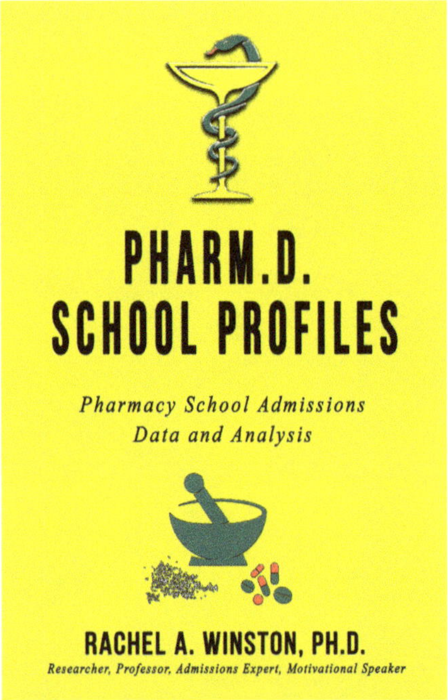

PHARM.D. SCHOOL PROFILES

Pharmacy School Admissions Data and Analysis

RACHEL A. WINSTON, PH.D.
Researcher, Professor, Admissions Expert, Motivational Speaker

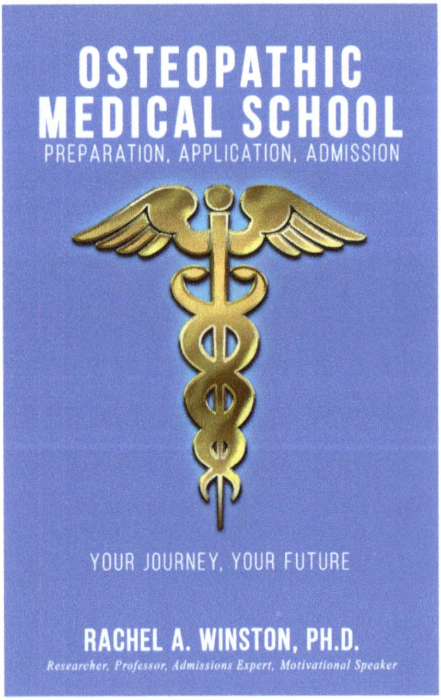

OSTEOPATHIC MEDICAL SCHOOL
PREPARATION, APPLICATION, ADMISSION

YOUR JOURNEY, YOUR FUTURE

RACHEL A. WINSTON, PH.D.
Researcher, Professor, Admissions Expert, Motivational Speaker

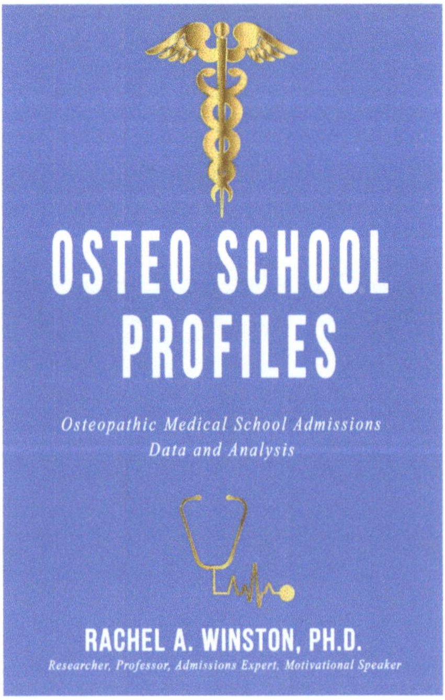

OSTEO SCHOOL PROFILES

Osteopathic Medical School Admissions Data and Analysis

RACHEL A. WINSTON, PH.D.
Researcher, Professor, Admissions Expert, Motivational Speaker

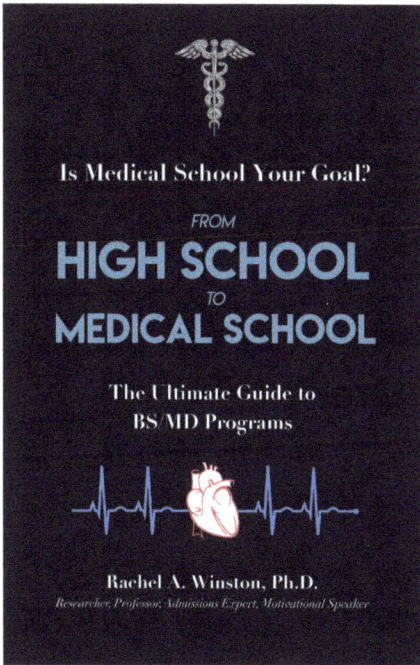

This comprehensive healthcare series is designed in full color to aid the growing number of applicants seeking clear, comprehensive materials. As a college admissions expert and former UCLA College Counseling Certificate Program faculty member, Dr. Winston is dedicated to helping students obtain the information they need.

FOR MORE INFORMATION

bsmdguide.com

medschoolexpert.com

Purchase books at Lizard-publishing.com

SERVICES OFFERED BY LIZARD EDUCATION:

- College Counseling
- Admissions News/Resources
- Essay Support and Editing
- Interview Preparation
- Road Trips to Visit Colleges
- Career Planning/Majors/Resumes
- BS/MD, BS/DO, BS/JD, BS/DDS
- Medical School
- Graduate School (Masters & Doctorate)
- Film Studio and Editing
- Portfolio Assistance/SlideRoom
- Athletics Recruiting/Highlight Films
- International Admissions/Visa/TOEFL
- Financial Aid and Scholarships
- UCs, Ivy Leagues, and Colleges Nationwide
- Book Publishing
- Engineering, Robotics, STEM
- Art Portfolios

Email: collegeguide@yahoo.com

Website: collegelizard.com

LIZARD

INDEX

Symbols

A

B

C

D

E

F

G

H

M

N

O

P

Q

R

S

T

U

V

W

Y

Z

www.ingramcontent.com/pod-product-compliance
Lightning Source LLC
Chambersburg PA
CBHW052016030426
42335CB00026B/3169